Kerry
Agent Orange
and an
American Family

Kerry
Agent Orange
and an
American Family

Clifford Linedecker
with Michael and Maureen Ryan

ST. MARTIN'S PRESS   NEW YORK

Copyright © 1982 by Cliff Linedecker, Michael Ryan
and Maureen Ryan
For information, write: St. Martin's Press,
175 Fifth Avenue, New York, N.Y. 10010
Manufactured in the United States of America

Library of Congress Cataloging in Publication Data

Linedecker, Clifford L.
Kerry, Agent Orange and an American family.

1. Ryan, Kerry. 2. Physically handicapped
children—United States—Biography. 3. Agent
Orange—Toxicology—United States. 4. Tetra-
chlorodibenzodioxin—Toxicology—United States.
5. Veterans—Diseases—United States. I. Title.
RD796.R93L56   362.4′3′0924 [B]   82–3171
ISBN 0–312–45112–1   AACR2

Design by Kingsley Parker

10 9 8 7 6 5 4 3 2 1

First Edition

Several persons in addition to those mentioned in the manuscript deserve recognition for their kind consideration and assistance in making this book possible. The author thanks: Attorney Anthony V. Curto, Terri Nedzveks, and Mary Benninghoff. Most of all my thanks go to my agent, the late Ruth Hagy Brod.

For him who shall have borne the battle,
and for his widow and his orphan.
—Slogan on the entrance
to the Veterans Administration
headquarters in
Washington, D.C.

CONTENTS

A section of photographs follows p. 112

PROLOGUE

Maureen Ryan shifted on the bed, rolling from her back onto her side. The baby had changed position and the expectant mother was vaguely uncomfortable, aware of a feeling similar to the sensation one experiences after overeating.

The movie date with friends had been her last planned night out before the baby arrived. The birth was scheduled for no more than seven or eight days in the future, and although she had enjoyed the movie, it had been tiring.

As they were driving home, Maureen and her husband discussed names again. If the child was a boy, there would be no question—he would be called Michael Francis Ryan, like his father, his grandfather, his great-grandfather, and other Ryan men before him.

And like the preceding generations of Ryan males, there would be no Juniors or Michael Francis Ryan IIs. It would be a plain and simple Michael Francis Ryan. And someday, also like the Michael Francis Ryans of County Limerick and of New York before him, he would inherit the family shillelagh, the gnarled, blackthorn walking stick with the initials M. F. R. carved on it, which had been handed down in the family from first son to first son for 200 years.

It was more difficult to settle on a name for a baby girl. Maureen had no special desire to pass on her own name, although ethnic Irish names like Bridget, Kitty, Mairead, Norah, Heather, and Colleen were mentioned from time to time. One of the more recent and intriguing suggestions was Kerrie. But whatever name was eventually selected, both Michael and Maureen had agreed that it should be relatively short and compatible with Ryan.

It was a little after midnight, January 23, 1971, and thoughts of babies and of names were beginning to fade as the young woman slipped into a dreamy state halfway between sleep and wakefulness. Beside her, her husband had already fallen asleep.

Their eyes snapped open almost simultaneously. A gray dampness was spreading between them, rapidly expanding and wetting the sheet.

"Oh my God," Michael yelled, instantly awake.

"It's broken. My water's broken," his wife murmured, speaking as much to herself as to her husband.

Michael leaped out of bed and grabbed the telephone. A moment later he lowered the receiver back onto the night table and turned to his wife. "I don't know the number," he confessed. She told him the number was scribbled on a piece of paper in her purse.

As her husband hurried outside to look for the purse, Maureen stepped into the shower. Moments later she heard a clatter as the contents of her purse were unceremoniously dumped onto the floor of the hallway.

Minutes after that the young couple's four-year-old Volkswagen pulled onto the Long Island Parkway, beginning a sixty-mile ride to Michael's parents' home in Brooklyn. Labor pains hadn't yet started and Maureen's obstetrician assured Michael during a hurried phone conversation that there was plenty of time. Her three older sisters had each already given birth to children and in each instance labor had been lengthy. That was comforting to know. Michael had once helped deliver a baby and it was an experience he didn't care to repeat with his wife.

Both husband and wife were, nevertheless, reasonably calm, considering the circumstances. They had handled the problem with the water as best they could by folding a sheet and placing it on the car seat under Maureen, but they were barely started before the water soaked through her slacks and the seat.

She was still losing fluid when Michael pulled the car to a stop in front of his parents' home about an hour later. Once they were inside, two more sheets were folded together and substituted for the first, which had been wet through. The new sheets were placed on a dining room chair for Maureen to sit on and were also quickly soaked.

Michael's mother was becoming quietly hysterical. Victoria, or Vicky, as she was more commonly known, had worked for twenty-five years as an obstetrical nurse, and she recognized polyhydrania when she saw it. The excessive loss of fluid was an unmistakable sign of trouble, an indication of an abnormal baby.

Vicky Ryan didn't wish to frighten either her son or her daughter-in-law, so she didn't say anything to them about her suspicions. Instead, she rode with them to Brooklyn Community Hospital, where she was head obstetrical nurse during the day shift. She calmly arranged for Maureen's admittance and began overseeing her care and preparation for the birth of the Ryan grandchild. But privately she confided to a night nurse that "it's not going to be a normal baby."

"Oh, come on, Ryan," the nurse replied. "You're just

being a nervous grandmother. You're worrying because it's your first grandchild."

It wasn't that at all. It was true that she hadn't yet helped deliver a grandchild, but during World War II she had helped two of her sisters deliver. Vicky Ryan loved her sisters, but when they were giving birth, she hadn't felt the same discomforting apprehension that had begun to steal over her when her daughter-in-law walked into her house earlier that evening.

When Dr. Milton Fritz, head of the hospital's obstetrical department and Maureen's personal obstetrician, walked into her room, the expectant grandmother repeated her fears. "It's going to be an abnormal baby," she quietly advised.

Shortly before Michael returned to his parents' home to wait with his father and sisters, his mother led him into Maureen's room. "Look at her stomach," she said, lifting the sheets. Maureen's stomach was flat, as if she weren't pregnant. Neither husband nor wife recognized the subtle warning of trouble ahead for what it was. Maureen smiled, proud of herself. It seemed that the exercises she had been practicing so faithfully during her pregnancy were paying off. Her body was retaining its slim appearance, and the baby hadn't even been born yet.

Maureen's labor was protracted and difficult. Her mother-in-law hovered over her for eighteen hours, closely monitoring the fetal heartbeat. It lingered comfortingly around a steady 140, never reeling into the precipitous drop to 110, 100 or below, which would indicate fetal distress. Vicky Ryan, nevertheless, continued to worry.

Nearly sixteen hours after her arrival at Brooklyn Community, Maureen was wheeled into the delivery room. It was almost 6 P.M. The nursing staff had changed shifts twice. Fatigue and worry had drawn gray pockets under the eyes of the veteran nurse who was watching over her.

The young woman had been in labor for hours, yet she was still losing fluid. More trouble developed when it was determined that the infant was in a posterior position, face up instead of face down as it should normally be. To further complicate the birth, the baby's head was large—like all Ryan children.

There was a whispered conference. Perhaps it might be best to perform a cesarean section, the obstetrician suggested. His nurse counseled against it. Since it was quite possible that the baby would be still born she was determined that if it was at all possible, her daughter-in-law would be spared surgery to remove the infant by cutting through the abdomen and womb.

Maureen had been given a paracervical block, a relatively mild anesthetic. Obstetricians at the hospital preferred their patients to be free of pain but conscious so that they could derive the greatest possible emotional satisfaction from the experience of giving birth. The patient was unaware that the procedure was other than routine when she was given additional medication that dropped her into a dreamy haze of morphia. Her mother-in-law was committed to protecting her. There would be need to cushion her from the initial shock of a less than perfect birth.

Maureen was semiconscious when she heard her mother-in-law gasp, "Oh my God, look at the baby's arm."

A moment later the hand of the anesthesiologist loomed over Maureen's face once more. It was cupping a mask. Shimmering and indistinct though it was, in Maureen's narcotic state it appeared huge. The hand and mask settled over her and she slipped deeply into unconsciousness.

The right arm was bowed back against the infant's side like a tiny bent chicken wing. X-rays would later disclose that there was a missing bone. The nurse was grief stricken as she peered through tear-dimmed eyes at her grandchild. She had helped deliver enough babies to know that if there was one birth defect, others were likely.

There was one comforting aspect to the troubled birth. The spirited squalling that reverberated through the delivery room provided unquestionable proof that at least the child's lungs were healthy.

The infant was a delicate, tiny girl who weighed a bare five pounds. Smaller children had been born and lived. That wasn't the problem. Vicky Ryan peered cautiously inside her granddaughter's mouth, half expecting to see a cleft palate. The mouth was perfect. The heartbeat also remained a sturdy 140. Then she turned the baby over. There was no rectum.

She turned to another nurse. "Baptize the baby," she said, and began to walk out of the delivery room.

"Where are you going?" the doctor asked.

"I'm going to call my son."

"Don't you think you should leave that to the doctor?"

"No way," she retorted.

Moments later Michael's sister, Patty, a student nurse, answered the telephone. Maureen's mother, sisters, and a brother-in-law had walked into the house moments before. Vicky's husband, Mick Ryan, had been out of bed at daybreak to begin cooking ham, turkey, and other food for members of the two families who gathered there throughout the day asking for news of the birth.

Patty's face brightened when she heard her mother's voice, and she signaled excitedly to others in the room. It had been a long labor. "Hey, Mom, did she have it?" she blurted.

"Put Michael on the phone," her mother demanded, ignoring the question and speaking gruffly to keep her voice steady.

"But Mom, a girl or a boy?" Patty persisted.

"Just put Michael on the phone," Vicky Ryan snapped.

Patty knew her mother well enough to realize that something was wrong. Sobered, she handed the telephone to her brother. Michael knew immediately there was trouble. Whatever had sobered his irrepressible sister had to be bad news.

Michael's forehead creased into an apprehensive frown as he picked up the receiver. He bent down toward it, handling it gingerly.

"Hello, Mom?" he ventured.

His mother's voice was cracked and unreal. "Hurry down here," she croaked. Then she lost her struggle against the emotions that were tearing her apart, and began to cry. Michael's mother wasn't a cryer—the Ryans had been taught that crying didn't solve problems—and Michael knew something had to be seriously wrong with either his wife or his baby.

"What's wrong?" he asked hoarsely.

"Just get down here," was the reply. The telephone clicked. His mother had hung up.

Michael's face lost its color as he turned to his sister. Patty felt the fear just as he did, but he needed comforting more than she.

"It's probably nothing terrible," she said, placing a reassuring arm around his shoulder. "Maybe the baby has a cleft palate . . . or a club foot . . ."

The suggestions were tentative, doubting, and she realized as she spoke that she wouldn't even have hinted at those possibilities if she hadn't feared something far worse.

As Michael and his father climbed into one car and members of Maureen's family jammed into another for the ride to the hospital, New York huddled under one of the fiercest snowstorms of the season. A piercing wind shrieked through the city canyons, hurling the falling snow at the caravan of cars as they raced through the streets. The few people on the streets hunched their backs against the cold.

Vicky Ryan was waiting at the door when the two cars pulled to a stop at the semiprivate rear entrance to the hospital. She told her son and Maureen's mother about the baby's deformities, but she didn't tell them the deformed arm and missing rectum might represent only the beginning of more trouble. The absence of a rectum and Maureen's persistent loss of fluid during labor made it almost certain that the little girl would have intestinal defects. And who knew what other problems might exist?

Vicky remained with the staff pediatrician as the examination of the baby continued. Michael walked outside to await his wife's arrival from the delivery room. He was shocked at her appearance. Her face seemed as white as the hospital gown she was wearing when she was wheeled past him, still unconscious, into her private room. He thought she looked like she was dying. He felt certain that he was going to lose both his wife and his baby.

When Maureen awakened, Michael was seated by her bed, holding her hand. Tears wet his cheeks as he told her that their baby was critically ill and might die. They hugged each other, sharing their grief. Then Maureen asked him to stay with the baby and make sure she was baptized. Exhausted, she drifted back to sleep.

Vicky Ryan had already asked one of the other nurses to phone for a staff pediatrician. He arrived minutes after the father and two grandmothers had viewed the infant in the nursery, and swiftly completed a preliminary examination. He was concerned about the heartbeat.

"Maybe it's a functional murmur," Vicky Ryan ventured, anxious to allay her own fears and the tentative prognosis of the pediatrician. A functional murmur would signify a heartbeat that was different but nonthreatening. It would not pose a serious health problem.

But the doctor shook his head. It was doubtful that the murmur was functional, he said. It would be cruel to deliberately raise false hopes.

If the baby was to have a chance to live, she would have to be transferred to another hospital with more specialized equipment and facilities for infants born prematurely or with life-threatening deformities. It was decided to take her to the Maimonides Medical Center in Brooklyn, a hospital with one of the best neonatal-care facilities in the country. The baby was placed in a portable incubator and readied for the trip.

Before the little girl was loaded into an ambulance, she was taken to her mother's room. The prognosis wasn't promising, and despite the superlative care available at Maimonides, there was grave doubt that she would live. Mrs. Ryan was determined that the infant's mother would hold the child in her arms at least one time. There might never be another opportunity. She took the baby from the incubator and handed her to Maureen. Silently Grandmother Ryan watched the brief communion between mother and daughter.

After the baby was replaced in the incubator and wheeled outside, the grandmother hesitated in the room. There was something she had to say. She had seen the families of other babies born crippled, mentally retarded, or in otherwise less than perfect health and condition, and had witnessed painful quarrels between grandparents, aunts and uncles, each side blaming the other for the trouble. The accusations and bitterness were senseless and cruel. They were cruelest of all to the stricken parents. She had resolved that the young woman whom she loved like another daughter wouldn't suffer that additional pain.

With her hands jammed into the pockets of her brown tweed coat, Vicky Ryan walked across the room and stood facing the window. Outside, the swirling snow diffused the lights from the vehicles and street lamps below, transforming them into splashes of gold, orange, and silver. When she spoke to Maureen, the words were forced out, but they were strong and clear:

"If any bastard tells you it was your fault, you tell him to deal with me! It is nothing you did, so get that through your head."

The ride to Maimonides was hectic, and did nothing to ease the tension. The blizzard was growing in intensity and the streets were almost impassable. The portly and aging ambulance driver had slipped in the snow, nearly dropping the incubator to the ground as it was being loaded into the ambulance. The infant's grandmother grabbed the incubator at the last moment and steadied it until the driver regained his balance. A well-intentioned young attendant who climbed into the back of the vehicle with Mrs. Ryan only added to her distress, cooing inanities about the "little snow princess" throughout the nervous ride.

With his mother-in-law as a passenger, Michael guided his tiny VW in a terrifying sprint through the snow-slickened streets, and was waiting at the hospital when the ambulance arrived.

Papers awaited Michael's signature authorizing his daughter's admittance to the hospital as well as emergency surgery. The initial procedure in the three-stage operation that was required would permit passage of digested food by enlarging the critically constricted opening that leads from the infant's stomach to the intestines.

The baby was taken immediately to surgery, where surgeons began cutting away deformed sections of her intestines and piecing back together the usable portions so that she would have a means of moving solid waste through her body. Her condition was too grave to immediately risk the sophisticated surgery necessary to reconstruct the missing rectum, so doctors performed a colostomy. It would provide a temporary means of eliminating body waste until she became strong enough to endure the more complicated procedure.

Later that night at his home, Michael knocked on the door of his sister Patty's bedroom. Inside, he slumped on the edge of her bed and began to cry. It was something she had never seen him do. A feeling of helplessness swept over Patty as she watched her brother's body shake with sobs. He was holding his head in his hands while the tears squeezed out between his fingers. His voice broke as he asked over and over, "Why me? What did I do?"

Three days later, as Maureen was being dismissed from the hospital, she was asked about the name to be entered on the baby's birth certificate. During the trauma and confusion of the birth, the task of selecting a name for the new child had been forgotten.

Maureen glanced at her husband, then back at the nurse. "Call her Kerrie," she said. "K-e-r-r-i-e." Startled, Michael's mother shook her head. "No, you can't spell it like that," she objected. "That was the name of the stripper at the 1939 World's Fair. It's got to be with a 'y' on the end." Maureen turned to the nurse and spelled the name out again. "K-e-r-r-y." The baby was named Kerry —as in County Kerry, Ireland.

1

FOUNDATIONS

Michael Francis Ryan and Daniel John O'Connor grew up in County Limerick, Ireland. They immigrated to the United States, married, served with distinction as U. S. Army military policemen during World War II, and returned to New York to raise families that one day would be linked by marriage.

Mick Ryan was a wiry, red-headed seventeen-year-old when he put together the money for passage and left the windy city of Limerick to board a ship bound for America. His only qualifications were good health, an alert, inquisitive mind, and a willingness to work at any honest job that would permit him to carve out a living for himself in his adopted country.

It was 1931, the Great Depression had begun, and it was a difficult time for anyone to be out of work—especially a young man who was not even a citizen and who had no job training. The occasional jobs that became available were usually reserved for native-born Americans or others who had immigrated years earlier.

Mick Ryan did what many jobless men and boys were doing in those days—he rode the rails looking for work.

Somewhere in the Midwest he was confronted by a rail-road bull with a gun and was thrown off the train. He landed hard and both his ankles snapped. He lay in pain beside the track for two days before he was found and given help.

Somehow, as other men did, he survived. He worked for a time in a canning factory in San Jose, California; worked as a laborer for Metro Goldwyn Mayer Studios; acted as an extra in Laurel and Hardy movies; was a crewman on a banana boat; and prospected for gold in Death Valley.

Five years after he began his wanderings, he returned east and became a naturalized American citizen. Some relatives on Long Island helped him to obtain work at a state psychiatric hospital in 1936. Three years later he met a pretty Scots-Irish nursing student, Victoria Molloy. They were married in 1940.

While America began to emerge from the Great Depression, much of the rest of the world was groaning under the first shocks of war. The year that Mick Ryan met his bride-to-be at King's Park, the German-Soviet nonagression pact freed Hitler to attack Poland. World War II had begun. Congress adopted the U.S. Selective Training and Service Act by the margin of one vote, and the law became effective on September 16, 1940. Mick Ryan enlisted in the Army. Despite his new status as a husband with family responsibilities, he left with pride for his year-long stint of military training.

On December 6, 1941, four days before his scheduled discharge from the service, he purchased civilian clothes. He would need the new clothes when he returned to his job at the hospital, he reasoned. The next day Pearl Harbor was bombed. It was nearly four years before he was to resume his former employment. In the interim, he served three years in the Pacific as a military policeman.

He was aboard ship in the convoy that launched the flight led by Colonel Jimmy Doolittle, which carried out the historic first bombing of Tokyo. He was a personal bodyguard to General Douglas MacArthur and participated in five campaigns before returning to the United States just prior to the general's triumphant return to the Philippines.

During the five years that Mick Ryan was in the Army, his wife was working at Brooklyn Community Hospital. For the first three years she worked twelve-hour nights, six nights a week, as nurse in charge of the obstetrical department. Some 6,000 babies were born there before she transferred to the neurosurgery department to work through the remaining years of the war.

Mick and Vicky Ryan conceived ten children. Only three, their first-born son, Michael Francis, and two daughters, Patty and Deirdre, survived. Mrs. Ryan had Rh-negative blood and developed antibodies against unborn male children who were Rh-positive, with the result that seven of the ten, including a set of twins, miscarried late in the pregnancies.

The children were raised in Irish Catholic neighborhoods of Flatbush, part of the multiethnic Brooklyn community whose 2.3 million people make it New York City's largest borough. The young Ryans were steeped in the culture of Ireland and imbued as well with an unquestioning love of their father's adopted country.

Many Irish are storytellers who have a vivid and loving familiarity with words, and Mick Ryan is one of these. Mealtimes and evenings were occasions for the children to sit at the dining room table and listen to stories of their father's youth when he stole hand grenades from the Black and Tans, the hated British occupiers. Or he would tell tales of the broad and shining River Shannon that flows so grandly past the old city of Limerick, or of spirits and banshees and family memories.

Vicky Ryan's stories were often of the babies she helped deliver—of breech births; cesarean sections; of happy parents; and all too often of puny, squalling, gray infants who were born addicted to the narcotics and prescription drugs abused by their mothers. To her husband, she sometimes confided amazement at the perfect health and condition of babies born to mothers who had used coat hangers, quinine, or powerful cathartics in dangerous and futile efforts to induce abortions.

There was no drinking in the Ryan household in Brooklyn. Mick Ryan has never forgotten how his father's unhappy bouts with the potent Irish home brew, poteen, and other forms of alcohol blighted his life and that of his family, and he neither smoked nor drank. He vowed, however, that he would take a drink the day he was presented with his first grandson and assured that the family name would be carried on.

Although conversation at the dinner table often drifted to Ireland, it was understood that the old-country history and captivating tales of ancient times applied only to the family's foundations and past. Both father and mother never failed to stress that the family's present, future, and loyalties belonged to the United States.

In 1955, when Michael was ten years old and he and his sisters were learning to love God, to be patriotic, to value education, and to think for themselves, American statesmen and military officials were arranging for U.S. troops to begin training soldiers of the South Vietnamese Army. Like most American families, the Ryans paid no more than passing attention to this detail of U.S. foreign policy.

Michael was sixteen and in high school in 1961 when American scientists from plant science laboratories at Fort Detrick, Maryland, began large-scale field tests to determine the most effective use of herbicides in Vietnam as a weapon of war. The U.S. Department of Agriculture, the U.S. Forest Service, and the armament laboratories at Eglin Air Force Base in Florida contributed scientists and other experts to the studies.

At the time, more than two-thirds of South Vietnam was covered by forests and dense, triple-canopied jungle. Destruction of selected areas of the forests would deny an enemy important cover and refuge which was being used to move supplies and as bases where troops could gather for attack.

A spraying program was personally approved by President John F. Kennedy. The Air Force responded quickly, and quite appropriately selected its Special Aerial Spray Flight for the job. The squadron had been flying insect spray missions in the United States and the Caribbean since the days of the Korean conflict. The new project was dubbed Operation Hades.

Michael had what he considered at the time to be more pressing concerns than events in Indochina. There were summers hanging out at the Sugar Bowl along the beach at Breezy Point, and the companionship of his friends. As he grew older, there was the added adventure and competition of chug-a-lugging beer with his buddies at the pubs.

He was from a family of swimmers and he continued working out in the ocean with his friends, usually at the beach off Breezy Point. Among his closest companions was Joe Carney, one of the country's leading half-milers. During the summer the two would swim together for four or five miles in the ocean and sometimes top off the exercise by running an equal distance along the beach. Almost all of Michael's summer companions were lifeguards or promising athletes.

Michael was nineteen and still enjoying the sun, ocean, and companionship at Breezy Point when North Vietnamese gunboats attacked two U.S. destroyers in the Gulf of Tonkin. On August 7, 1964, Congress approved the Tonkin Gulf Resolution authorizing presidential action that paved the way for a massive step-up in the American military role in Vietnam.

While Michael and his sisters were growing up in Brooklyn, Daniel O'Connor's children were also being raised in New York City, but more than twenty miles away in the Bronx.

Daniel O'Connor married and started his family sooner than his fellow townsman, Mick Ryan. His first child, Helen, named for her mother, was born in 1938. By the time he entered the Army during World War II and was sent to Europe as a military policeman, he and his wife were the parents of two more girls, Carol and Lorraine.

A well-built 195-pound six-footer who smiled often and laughed easily, Daniel could be serious and quietly courageous when circumstances called for it. By the time he left Europe to return to the United States, he had been awarded two Bronze Stars for valor, one earned during the Normandy Invasion, and the other at the Battle of the Bulge.

The next child born to the O'Connors, some three years after the war, was another girl, given the classic Irish name, Maureen. Two more girls, Bernadette and Gail, and three boys, Danny, John, and Brian, eventually swelled the O'Connor brood to nine. There was a span of nineteen years between the ages of the oldest and the youngest.

Maureen was quickly nicknamed "Mickey" by her father, because of her Irish temper. When it flared, the veins in her neck stood out and Daniel O'Connor laughed and compared his daughter to an Irish truck driver. "You look like a Mick," he teased. That always made the veins pop out another centimeter.

Maureen was the first of the children Daniel could watch grow up from infancy. He had missed the early childhood of his older girls because of the war. And understandably he tended to spoil his hot-tempered, auburn-haired daughter. In return, she idolized him.

Daniel was protective of all his daughters, but when he was dealing with them, he also practiced an egalitarianism rare for the times. They were taught always to take pride in themselves and to aspire to any ambition they desired. Daniel believed that no opportunity should be denied to them on the basis of sex discrimination. Sometime before his boys were born, a church organization he belonged to sponsored a father-son banquet. He showed up with his girls.

The children were always aware of the close bond between their parents. Their father worked days as manager of an A & P supermarket and their mother worked as a self-trained accountant from 4 PM to midnight, and the girls grew accustomed to seeing their father leaning far out of the fire escape window late at night, watching for his wife to come home. On the nights he was too exhausted to stay awake, he always left a note on the kitchen table telling her that fresh doughnuts and milk were in the refrigerator—and that he loved her. The O'Connor youngsters grew up believing that the love so openly expressed between their parents existed in every family.

Maureen was thirteen years old and in the eighth grade at St. Joseph's parochial school when her father died suddenly. Daniel O'Connor had begun complaining of stomach pains, and he wasn't a man given to complaining about trifles. A week later he was dead of cancer of the pancreas.

Mrs. O'Connor was left with nine children, eight of

them still at home. The youngest was two. Devastated as she was over her father's death, when Maureen learned there was a $10,000 insurance policy, she was certain the family had been left secure. She believed they could live forever on $10,000. Then a week after Mr. O'Connor's death, fire swept through the house, burning the family out of their home.

An erect, regal woman with a strong sense of self, Helen O'Connor had a fierce pride in her family. She was independent and confident of her own abilities to raise her children in a manner her husband would have been proud of. Mrs. O'Connor was also a gritty, practical woman, and after the fire she applied most of her husband's $10,000 insurance money to the purchase of a house in Yorktown Heights, an affluent suburban community in Westchester County. The house was near the home of her husband's brother. Drawing on her inner strength, she extended her workday from 9 AM to 9 PM, toiling six-day weeks to provide for her family.

Rigorous discipline and hard work were cornerstones of life in the O'Connor home, and each member of the household learned early to assume responsibility and to carry their own weight. As the older daughters left home to marry, the chore of caring for younger siblings was passed down until it was Maureen's turn. She routed her younger brothers and sisters out of bed in the mornings, fed them, and sent them to school.

As they became old enough, all the children held after-school and summer jobs. Maureen became accustomed to hurrying home from classes at St. Joseph's, and later at St. Helena's High School, to fix supper for the younger children and for her mother, doing what housework she could, then rushing off to a job as a checker at the A & P, or later as a salesgirl in a ladies' clothing store. None of the children ever questioned her authority. It was understood that it was the responsibility of the eldest to take care of the youngest while their mother was working. Everyone kept too busy to get into trouble. Life in the O'Connor household wasn't easy, but the adversity was molding strong characters. The children were being taught to be survivors.

Grocery shopping was done by Mrs. O'Connor on Saturday nights after work. All day Sunday she washed and ironed clothes. Education was important to the O'Connors, as it was to the Ryans, and despite the financial strain, Maureen's mother explained that she was prepared to help put her through college or nursing school. But money was dear and the one restriction Mrs. O'Connor tried to impose on her daughter was a promise that once she started classes she wouldn't quit.

Still a teenager, Maureen hadn't yet decided what she wished to do with her life. She couldn't promise that she wouldn't drop out of school. So one day in June 1966, shortly before graduation from St. Helena's, she rode a subway from the Bronx to Park Avenue in Manhattan, where she took a preemployment physical at IBM Corporation. She was seated in a waiting room with several other young men and women, modestly clutching the slit back of a paper gown when Michael Ryan walked inside. He was similarly dressed.

Michael's parents had been urging him to become a lawyer, and the idea appealed to him. After graduation from high school, he had started part-time classes in pre-law at the downtown Brooklyn campus of St. John's University. Like the others seated self-consciously in the huge waiting room, he was at IBM to take a preemployment physical.

Maureen was a strikingly pretty redhead with fine, cleanly sculpted features and radiant blue eyes. Michael Ryan was impressed.

2

A SECRET
SHARED

The second time Michael saw Maureen she was working as a receptionist and he was a mail clerk. Starched and tidy, she was seated at her typewriter diligently typing a letter.

"Did you get a load of the new receptionist?" Michael grinned at a buddy when he returned to the mail room. "She's not too bad."

His friend slipped into the office to look for himself. A few minutes later he returned to the mail room shaking his head negatively from side to side. He was looking at Michael as if he pitied him for betraying such obvious bad taste. "She's a dog," he advised.

Michael was puzzled. He couldn't believe they were talking about the same girl. The riddle was solved a few days later when he learned that his friend had himself asked the receptionist for a date. The mail-room lothario gloated and bragged for an entire day until he had to cancel his plans unexpectedly.

Michael seized his opportunity. He began to take his time when he delivered mail to Maureen's office and devoted considerable attention to teasing and entertaining

her with stories and jokes. Maureen enjoyed the attention, and she especially liked Michael's flair for comedy.
In many ways it mirrored her own.

Then she met Patty. Michael's sister began stopping off
occasionally at the IBM offices to have lunch or to ride the
subway home with her brother. She would wait for him
in the reception room and quickly developed a close
friendship with Maureen. Maureen soon began visiting
Patty's home and accompanying her to other places
where the Ryan teenagers gathered. Her acquaintance
with Michael remained casual until the summer night she
was seated outside a beachside restaurant watching the
ocean and he walked by with a group of friends. He
stopped abruptly, grinned, and announced matter-of-
factly, "Someday I'm going to marry you."

Soon after that they began dating, and Maureen began
seeing as much of Michael as she saw of Patty during her
overnight visits to the Ryan home. Invariably, a few minutes after the older Ryans had excused themselves and
gone upstairs to bed, Patty would slip into her own room
leaving her brother and her girlfriend alone.

Mick Ryan was a strict disciplinarian, and Michael knew
him well enough to realize there would be serious trouble
if his father caught him necking with Maureen on the sofa.
So he booby-trapped the hallway outside his parents' bedroom with buckets and broom handles.

Michael's life became a combination of work at IBM,
classes at St. John's, and trips to the O'Connor home at
night and on weekends for dates with Maureen. His aca-
demic performance, already less than inspired, began to
slide. One of the activities had to be sacrificed. He began
dropping classes one by one until there was none left to
drop. He quit school.

In 1964 the O'Connor family had returned to an apartment in the Bronx. The hours of commuting from York-

town Heights five times a week stacked onto her long working day had become too much for Mrs. O'Connor. The Bronx, home of Yankee Stadium and the world-famous Bronx Zoo, was a borough of some 1.3 million ethnically diverse people. Streets were faced with tidy woodframe and brick houses and neatly kept apartment buildings. Every dozen blocks or so, there was a church and usually a school.

Maureen's neighborhood in the South Bronx had not yet given in to the encroaching desolation and street crime that would mark the borough by the 1970s. The O'Connor children didn't have keys to their apartment. The front door was never locked because no one worried about burglars. During the summer the girls and their friends sunbathed unmolested, on "Tar Beach," the tarred roof of their apartment building.

Michael was enjoying his life too much to take serious notice of how the military draft and enlistments were thinning out the young men in his Brooklyn neighborhood. A few acquaintances had already entered the service, but he hadn't seen much of them recently anyway. Most of his free time was spent with Maureen.

Nevertheless, it wasn't much of a surprise when his mother walked into her bedroom where he was napping one day and dropped an envelope on his face. "They gotcha," she said.

He didn't bother to open the letter, merely felt for the subway token inside. Then he rolled over and went back to sleep. It was October 1965. His induction notice had arrived on his parents' twenty-fifth wedding anniversary. He was twenty years old.

It was still early in America's involvement in the fighting in Vietnam, and despite growing opposition elsewhere, most of the young men conscripted from the country's working-class families accepted military service as a duty expected of them. U.S. forces in Vietnam had by this time reached 184,000, and the young men who were serving there were considered by most Americans to be patriots. There were as yet no horror stories of GIs becoming junkies, no fragging or murders of unpopular officers, and only a small antiwar movement. "The Ballad of the Green Beret" would become a hit record, and a John Wayne movie about the elite corps of Army professionals would draw huge crowds to theaters and make the job of Army recruiters easier. The President and Congress had determined that it was necessary for a selected few of the nation's young men to be given military training and for some of them to be sent to fight in Southeast Asia. Now it was Michael's turn, and he went.

Michael wasn't enthusiastic about leaving Maureen and his family to become an Army private, but he wouldn't be Mick Ryan's son if he shirked. Furthermore, two years of military service might provide the time and opportunity for him to develop concrete career plans.

Maureen thought she and Michael would have a quiet romantic evening together before he marched off to war. But even the best of plans sometimes go awry.

One of Michael's friends from the neighborhood, Billy Gibson, was inducted the same day as he. On the last Saturday before the draftees left home for induction, they were guests of honor at a neighborhood party in the Ryan home. It was three days after the first massive electrical failure and blackout had darkened New York and additional large areas of the East Coast.

The day of the party, Mick Ryan was up early to cook food for friends and relatives of the two recruits. One of the most popular guests was Michael's cousin Donald. Donald was in his mid-twenties and had recently been honorably discharged after serving an enlistment in the Army that included service in the Special Forces. He told Michael at the party that he was planning to reenlist. It wasn't surprising. Michael had always admired his older cousin's scrappy adventurousness. When he was a boy, Donald went out of his way to protect younger, more defenseless children from bullies.

The guests also included the Listons, longtime friends who had known Michael's father in Ireland. One of the Liston boys brought a bugle, one brought a guitar, and two others carried bagpipes into the house. Their sister, Helen, had a sweet soprano voice, and the family helped keep the party lively, singing and playing spirited Hibernian tunes like "Johnny, I Hardly Knew Ye," "Gary Owen," "The Patriot Game," and other ballads recalling the heritage of the Irish people.

The party goers finally formed a line and paraded out the door with Donald in the lead and the pipers and bugler close behind. They snake-walked through the streets, heading toward Flatbush Avenue, playing and singing "Gary Owen" while Michael and Billy accepted the congratulations and good wishes of their neighbors.

Monday morning Billy's father, a New York City police lieutenant, drove the two draftees to the Whitehall Induction Station on his way to work.

Maureen and Patty decided a short time later to go to the induction center to say goodbye one more time to Michael and Billy. They talked their way past the first sentry by telling him they had an important message to deliver to Patty's brother. A moment later they were confronted by a sergeant who was one of the tallest, huskiest men they had ever seen. A wary veteran of duty there, he was experienced enough not to be taken in by their story of an important message to be delivered to one of the inductees. He also refused their request to use the restroom and was about to escort them outside when they broke away and bolted for the stairs. He lumbered after them but stopped when they ran inside the ladies' room.

The sergeant was trying to decide what to do when he was called away. Before leaving, he cracked the door open and whispered orders for them to stay where they were until he returned.

The teenagers immediately slipped outside and began searching the induction center for Michael and Billy. They found them seated with a large group of other young men in a third-floor classroom. Michael's eyes widened when he saw them. Then he slumped in his chair. A moment later the huge hands of the sergeant closed on the backs of the girls' necks and they were unceremoniously escorted outside the building. The sergeant was furious. "Never before in the history of the Whitehall has a woman entered these halls," he roared.

The girls were persistent and they refused to give up. They waited until the inductees boarded buses outside the building, then hailed a cab.

"There's five dollars in it for you—follow that bus," Maureen yelled at the cabbie. It was the beginning of a mad race behind a caravan of Army buses winding through the streets of lower Manhattan. The race ended at Penn Station, where Maureen and Patty were finally able to say their last goodbyes.

Before beginning basic—and later, advanced combat training—at Fort Hood, Texas, Michael had taken a battery of written examinations. He was advised by his captain that his test scores were high enough to qualify him for preparatory training and entry into the U.S. Army Military Academy at West Point. Acceptance would mean a minimum eight-year commitment, four years for schooling at the Academy and four years of active Army service. Michael rejected the offer. As a boy he had once dreamed of West Point, but after a few days in the Army, he had experienced enough marching, close-order drill, inspections, and scrubbing of barracks floors to lose interest permanently in a military career.

Two days before Christmas Michael and four of his buddies from Brooklyn were sitting in the Fort Hood Post Exchange with five-day passes, drinking beer and debating how they could get home. There was no point in attempting to catch military standby seats on airplanes sometimes allocated to servicemen on a reduced fare basis, because of the heavy holiday travel. There weren't any to be obtained. The only seats available were first class, and they were too expensive.

When the recruits walked out of the PX, they were defeated. They had been unable to devise a plan to get them home for the holiday, so they hailed a taxi to drive them back to the barracks.

"Where to?" the cabbie asked.

"Brooklyn," Michael said.

"Brooklyn where?"

"Brooklyn, New York City."

No one was laughing at Michael's joke. They were as dejected as he was. But they straightened up in their seats and listened when they heard the cab driver's reply.

"Okay, that'll cost you five hundred," he said.

Michael could hardly believe he had heard correctly. The cab driver was serious.

"Four hundred," Michael countered.

The cabbie agreed to drive the GIs the 1,800 miles to Brooklyn for four hundred fifty dollars—ninety dollars each.

Somewhere in Arkansas the cabbie fell asleep and nearly wrecked the taxi. His passengers began to trade off driving after that, but the cabbie was at the wheel when the cab rode across the Verrazano Narrows Bridge and into the city some thirty-four hours after leaving the base.

Michael was the last of the group to be dropped off, and when the taxi pulled up in front of his house, his father ran outside to greet him. It was Christmas Eve and Michael's return was the best present he could have asked for. If his son had written that he planned to fly home for the holidays, Mick Ryan would have been more than happy to meet him at the airport and drive him to Brooklyn.

"Don't worry, Michael," he said, crinkling his eyes with happiness as he pulled open the door of the cab with one hand and reached for his billfold with the other. "I'll get the bill."

Mick Ryan's startled expression when the cabbie asked for ninety dollars was almost worth the sprint home. Michael happily paid his own cab fare and added a tip.

A couple of hours later Michael was in the Bronx knocking at the door of the O'Connor apartment. The day after Christmas he boarded an airplane at JFK International Airport and flew back to Texas.

After completion of training at Fort Hood, he was assigned to the Eleventh Armored Cavalry, the proud "Black Horse Regiment" at Fort Meade, Maryland. Soon the Army decided it was time to send the Eleventh Armored Cavalry to Vietnam.

In April 1966 the North Vietnam Press Agency broadcast charges from Joseph Mary Ho Hua Ba, Catholic representative of the National Liberation Front, that babies were being killed by herbicide and defoliant spray directed on jungles and food crops by American forces and the South Vietnamese government. The broadcast was monitored by Reuters, the British press agency, and the charges were disseminated worldwide.

Michael was selected with about 150 other officers and enlisted men as part of an advance party to be flown to Vietnam to prepare a camp for the rest of the regiment. The advance party was scheduled to leave on August 6, 1966.

Michael and Maureen had been expecting his orders to Vietnam, and dreading it. Their previous separations were nothing compared to the plight they would be in once he was overseas. Maureen decided that it was time for them to get married.

It had been understood that they would marry someday, but they were waiting, respecting the wishes of their parents that they first further their education and establish a strong financial, emotional, and spiritual base for their lives together. Vietnam changed all that.

At that time in the state of New York, men had to be twenty-one to marry without parental consent. Women could marry when they were eighteen. Nearly three years younger than her boyfriend, Maureen was already of legal age to marry. But it was early July, and Michael wouldn't be twenty-one until the twenty-fifth of the month. Maureen forged his baptismal certificate. (His birth certificate was a Xerox copy and couldn't be altered, but information on the baptismal document was filled in with ink.) She changed the date of birth on the certificate from 7-25-45 to 6-25-45. Then she and Michael took the document with them to City Hall, and she paid for the license. Michael was almost broke and had only seven dollars. It was barely enough to get him back to Fort Meade.

But Maureen had been saving her money and talking to her girlfriends. Her older sisters were married, and she was familiar with the legal process. Leafing through the yellow pages of a telephone book, she located the name of a judge in Yonkers. She telephoned him and explained that her boyfriend was in the Army and scheduled to be shipped to Vietnam. She asked if the judge would marry them. He would.

That weekend when Michael left the base on a forty-eight hour pass, he traveled straight home, dressed in his father's best suit and sneaked out of the house. He was in good physical condition when he was drafted, but the Army training and the reasonably regular hours he was required to observe had left him even more trim than before. He had dropped ten pounds or more to a lanky 168 on a five-foot, ten-inch frame, and he no longer fit into his old clothes.

For her wedding dress Maureen selected a neatly tailored, chocolate skirt-and-blouse set that belonged to her sister Bernadette. She pulled her shoulder-length auburn hair back in a pony tail and wound it over rollers to give the impression of more height. It was a popular style.

Tommy Portogallo, another Brooklyn draftee, had become Michael's closest friend in the Army and was the best man. Michael and Tommy drove to Maureen's apartment to pick her up for the ride to the judge's home. Maureen gasped when they walked in. The best man was impeccably dressed in a tailored black suit. The groom's rumpled suit looked terrible. The sleeves of his jacket dangled almost to his knuckles, and only the creases and rumples in his trousers prevented his pants legs from dragging along the floor. Maureen's eyebrows wrinkled into a disappointed frown. At her suggestion Michael walked into a bedroom, climbed out of his suit, and waited while she pressed it for him.

At 5 PM they were standing side by side in the living room of the judge's home in Yonkers repeating their marriage vows. Maureen was afraid to tell her sisters and girlfriends, including Patty, about the wedding, so there was no maid of honor. The judge's wife served as a witness. It was six days before Michael's twenty-first birthday.

Throughout the ceremony Tommy moaned about Michael's father. "Oh my God," he groaned, "do you know what he's gonna do to you if he finds out? Oh is he gonna be mad!"

Tommy's fears were justified. Michael was well aware of how upset his parents would be when they realized they would never be able to help plan or witness the wedding of their only son. Mick Ryan's eyes would narrow and the veins in his neck would bulge in anger. Vicky Ryan would probably cry.

Maureen was also nervous and doing her best to disregard the feeling of guilt that nagged at her. She had never before done anything behind her mother's back. Once the secret was out, there would be damaged feelings at the O'Connor household just as there would be at the Ryan home.

But those problems would have to be faced later. After the vows were said, they thanked the judge, said goodbye to Tommy, and checked into a motel. Maureen had an 11 PM curfew.

When Michael kissed her goodnight at her door, a few minutes before 11 P.M., he was favoring a swollen and lacerated lip. When he had switched off the light a few minutes after checking into the motel, he groped his way across the room and tripped over the rug. Pitching forward, he had struck his mouth on his bride's knee.

There were other weekends together before the scheduled departure for Vietnam. They were less nervous, but the tension created by their deception remained. The couple finally revealed their secret to Patty. She was horrified. "Why did you have to tell me?" she wailed. The next instant she was pleading with them. "Oh promise me, promise you'll give me some warning before you tell my parents. I want to be out of the state."

The departure date for Vietnam was finally set for August 11. On August 6 Michael obtained another pass and he and Maureen were able to spend one more weekend together. It was the same weekend that the news media provided front-page and television coverage of the wedding of Luci Baines Johnson and Patrick Nugent. Michael and Nugent were about the same age. But Michael was going to Vietnam, and the President's new son-in-law was not.

Five days later Michael telephoned Maureen from a phone booth at Fort Meade. They could hardly hear each other over the roar of helicopter engines in the background. Shortly after that Michael carried his rifle, field pack, and other equipment aboard an Air Force Globemaster at a nearby Air Force base. The giant aircraft was loaded with trucks, tanks, jeeps, and some 300 men—including the Eleventh Cavalry's advance party and replacement soldiers assigned to other regiments— when it took off on the flight to Vietnam.

The Globemaster made refueling stops in Alaska and Japan before the men and equipment were unloaded at Tan Son Nhut Air Force Base a few kilometers outside Saigon. Members of the advance party were issued live ammunition for their rifles, and within an hour after arriving in Vietnam, they were in trucks being driven into the field.

3

WALKING PNEUMONIA

While the main contingent of the Eleventh Armored Cavalry prepared to leave for Vietnam by ship, Michael Ryan and other members of the advance party were constructing a base camp at Long Binh just above the lush river delta some twenty miles north of Saigon.

Tents were erected, boardwalks installed, and latrines built. Guard towers, bunkers, and a communications center were constructed. Trees and other vegetation on the camp site and along the base perimeters were chopped down and bulldozed. GIs followed up from the backs of tanker trucks, directing clouds of blue-gray spray from huge hoses attached to fifty- and one-hundred-gallon drums at the surviving undergrowth. The trucks rumbled along the edges of the base a half dozen times during the five weeks the advance party worked to prepare Long Binh for the arrival of the main force of 3,000 men.

Denuding of the perimeter was an important factor in base security. The vegetation was cleared for some one hundred meters, eliminating enemy cover and providing a clear field of fire for the defenders in case Long Binh was attacked. Michael walked the perimeter many nights on guard duty and it was always quiet. As soon as the clouds of spray settled, the noise of insects and birds ceased. Plant life died, leaving ferns, flowers and grass burned, twisted, and lifeless. The sprayed area was a dead zone.

The spray was evil smelling and cloyingly sweet. It clung to the air like mold and attached itself with fungus-like tenacity to whatever it touched. In clear weather diaphanous gray mists from the spraying sometimes brushed the newly erected tents with a thin, dull coating of dust.

Michael wasn't very concerned about the spray. He assumed that it was a mixture of oil and water, or some other substance used to keep the dust down and retard plant growth. Nor did anyone else appear to worry much about it. The soldiers who handled it weren't especially careful, and it was frequently spilled or sprayed on their clothing, their bodies, and on their equipment.

Most of the soldiers were content to do their jobs and count the days until their tours in Vietnam were over. Other things appeared to be much more worrisome or threatening than the spray the Army manuals described as a powerful chemical herbicide that was "relatively non-toxic to man or animals."

The GIs were assured there was no danger to them in Vietnam from the air. American forces ruled the skies. The danger at that time, the soldiers were told, was from the little men in black pajamas who hid in and fought from the jungles—the Viet Cong. Long Binh was reasonably secure, and members of the advance party occupied themselves with the job of preparing for the arrival of the regiment's main contingent.

It was hot, heavy work. The advance party arrived during the monsoon, when it rained almost continuously from sodden, slate-gray skies. Despite the rain the heat clung oppressively to the soldiers like a heavy film. There was nowhere to go to get away from it.

After a few minutes of work, the rain or their own sweat soaked the soldiers through and plastered their clammy camouflage utilities and olive fatigues to their skin. Bodies dehydrated rapidly when it wasn't raining, and the GIs learned to hold their canteens at the bottom edge of the steeply sloping tops of the tents to catch runoff water for drinking. They were aware that tropical diseases could be transmitted by organisms in the water, and they were usually careful to drop a few chlorination tablets inside before drinking. The established ratio of tablets for a given amount of water was recommended in Army training manuals.

At other times they caught runoff water to bathe in, using their helmets as washbasins or tubs as soldiers have done in a half-dozen previous wars. The technique was simple enough. The helmet would be filled with water, some soap added, and the GI would clean himself from top to bottom, usually beginning with a shave.

Tanker trucks later provided plenty of water for the armored cavalrymen. It was pretreated with chemicals or was otherwise considered safe for drinking and cooking in. There were other reasons why it was considered to be an improvement over the runoff water; it was clear and wasn't filled with the tiny organisms usually so visible in the water caught from the surface of the tents.

Michael was trim and in excellent physical condition when he was flown to Vietnam, and initially the hard work and the heat didn't bother him. Very soon, however, he began to show signs of debilitation. He was constantly exhausted, he developed headaches that were so severe they made him nauseous, he was short of breath and his chest throbbed with pain. His neck and body broke out in pimples that swelled into ugly pus-filled sores. The rash was especially tormenting along the insides of both thighs. It was painful for him to walk because his clothing would rub against the sores, breaking them and causing them to bleed or seep pus. He lost his appetite, and his weight dropped so rapidly that after a few days he could hardly keep his pants up. He took in his belt a half-dozen notches.

Five weeks after Michael's arrival the main body of the Black Horse Regiment splashed into the camp through the mud and rain. The men arrived in trucks, armored personnel carriers, tanks and jeeps. Tommy Rafferty, a soldier from Brooklyn whom he had met during their induction together, was the first person Michael saw whom he recognized.

But Rafferty hardly recognized Michael. "Oh, hell," he groaned to a sergeant as he recognized the emaciated and listless GI in front of him, "if this is what Vietnam did to Ryan in five weeks, I'm sure not staying here a year. You can take me to the stockade right now."

But Rafferty stayed in Vietnam for a full tour of duty, and Michael reported for sick call. He was hospitalized for ten days. Medics injected him with massive doses of penicillin and advised him that he had walking pneumonia. His weight had plummeted to 128 pounds, fully clothed and holding an M-16 rifle.

Respiratory disease among American troops was common in Southeast Asia, despite the tropical temperatures. As well as being hot, the climate was either extremely dry or extremely wet, depending on whether or not it was the monsoon season. Soldiers suffered from swollen mucous membranes irritated by the dust during the dry season, and from moisture during the monsoon.

The first night Michael was in the field hospital, a soldier in the bunk underneath his and a wounded soldier across the aisle from him died. Michael's new bunkmate had malaria and constantly shook, vomited, and complained of alternating fevers and chills. Malaria had developed into a major health problem for American troops in Vietnam. It was especially virulent and widespread in the field and jungle areas, where mosquito carriers bred in the billions and were impossible to control.

Michael had thrown away his malaria pills. His father had refused to take preventive medication to protect him from malaria while he was in New Guinea during World War II, and he was the only man in his outfit who didn't contract the disease. Michael also rejected his daily dosage of chloroquine and, like his father, avoided the disease as handily as he avoided the medication.

Michael was sick enough without suffering from malaria. Even after he was discharged from the hospital and returned to his company, he was excused from duty for another ten days and spent most of the time in his bunk coughing up evil-tasting fluids. He was devoid of energy.

If other members of the advance party were hospitalized for walking pneumonia or similar ailments, Michael didn't know about it. The men in the advance party had been plucked from various units and returned to their own companies when the full regiment arrived at Long Binh, so he lost contact with them.

As the Black Horse Regiment was digging in at Long Binh, some seven miles away near Bien-Hoa, another spunky soldier from New York who had already served one tour in Vietnam as a Green Beret was doing his second hitch as a medic with the 173rd Airborne Brigade. John Woods was married and had two healthy daughters, but he had chosen to reenlist in the Army and volunteered for Vietnam, where he knew he was needed.

Bien-Hoa was between Saigon and the Ho Chi Minh Trail, which the enemy used to transport men and supplies from the north. Woods also observed chemical defoliants being sprayed on nearby jungle and along base perimeters, usually from HU-1 helicopters or fixed-wing aircraft. Like Michael Ryan, he was frequently assigned to perimeter security. But as a medic, he also accompanied troops into the field, often into recently defoliated areas of the jungles. In the target areas, Air Force C-123 *Providers* and the older C-47 cargo planes that had been converted into spray aircraft left almost total devastation in their wake.

The *Providers* were not designed for combat, but for cargo and troop transport. Spray booms equipped with sixteen nozzles each were mounted under each wing. A gasoline engine, usually twenty horsepower, was added to pump the chemical through pressurized hoses from the tank to wing racks. The spray planes were operated by three-man crews, except for the lead plane on each mission, which carried a navigator to direct the flight to targets.

Traveling at about 130 knots, barely above stalling speed for the twin-engine C-123s, the aircraft would swoop down to treetop level—about 150 feet—to loose their frothy white clouds of defoliant along communication lines and at jungle canopy suspected of providing cover for Viet Cong or for their food and weapons caches.

The low-level flying invited attack by the enemy, and the aircraft returned from almost every mission with bullet holes. But higher altitudes would have prevented the defoliant from settling on the foliage in sufficient strength to be maximally effective. Spraying at a height lower than 150 feet would cause overkill and waste of the expensive chemical. The cost of an average load of 11,000 pounds was $5,000.

The C-123s carried single 1,000-gallon chemical tanks, added and adapted from B-50s, in their bellies. The spray was controlled by an operator who sat inside an armor-

plated box near the rear cargo door. There he could monitor a pump that forced the thick, oily, brown chemical out
of dispensing tubes at the rate of four gallons per second
when the pilot triggered a release. An experienced crew
needed only four minutes to loose enough defoliant to kill
every bit of foliage over a 300-acre area.

Army helicopters converted for spraying by the attach-
ment of gravity-feed sprayers and 200-gallon fuel tanks,
only half filled because of weight limitations, could drop
as low as 100 feet and fly at a slower fifty-five knots. They
were often used when friendly villages were too near
areas to be defoliated to make spraying from the C-123s
safe. Cargo doors were removed from the helicopters so
that gunners could return ground fire; the propellers
kicked up whirlpools of the spray, blowing it back into the
faces of the crew. Spray that spilled onto the fuselage was
known to peel the paint off.

Although four different chemical mixtures were used,
the most common tree defoliant was called Agent Orange. The name derived from the color-coded stripes
painted on the fifty-five gallon drums it was transported
in. Agent Orange was composed of equal parts of two
chemicals known as 2,4,5-T and 2,4-D.

Agent Blue, a solution of cacodylic acid, which is more
than fifty percent arsenic and nonselectively kills green-
leaf and herblike plants, was used on rice paddies.
Agent Blue was the chief crop killer in the Free World
arsenal.

Agent White was a solution mixed with principal components of picloram, a selective herbicide most effective
on broadleaf plants, and 2,4-D. It was known to have high
solubility in water and high stability in soil. Consequently
there was a strong possibility of its movement in surface
and drainage water.

Agent Purple was a mixture of 1,4-D and a slightly

different form of 2,4,5-T than that used in Agent Orange, which had begun replacing it in 1964.

Jungle, highways, communications lines, and base perimeters where soldiers like Michael Ryan and John Woods worked and fought were the main targets of the herbicides and defoliants, but helicopters and fixed-wing aircraft also sprayed the chemical on rice, melon, bananas, breadfruit, mango, and other crops so they could not be used to feed the enemy. Waterways were also sprayed from the air and from boats.

The program called for full payment to Vietnamese peasants for lost crops. Unfortunately all or large portions of the payments often wound up in the hands of avaricious province chiefs and subchiefs. Red tape discouraged many other peasants, who couldn't cope with the bureaucrats they had to deal with to acquire certification of damages from the central government.

The practice of spraying food crops was so politically delicate that many key missions had to be approved by some of the highest authorities in the U.S. Embassy, the Republic of Vietnam, and military forces of both governments. The procedures were carefully outlined in formal instructions referred to as Project Farmgate. Most spraying missions by fixed-wing aircraft required formal requests from local American and South Vietnamese army commanders, which moved to the Saigon headquarters of the U.S. Army, through American intelligence and to the U.S. Embassy, as well as to senior officials of the South Vietnamese government. Individual province chiefs were also consulted. Military commanders submitted individual overlays or photographs depicting areas to be sprayed. Approval usually required waits of 90 to 180 days.

Since requests passed through so many levels in the chain of command of both the American military and the South Vietnamese government, the enemy was usually aware well ahead of time when spray planes were scheduled to appear over target areas.

Accidents and mistakes occurred frequently. Spray was sometimes caught in the winds and drifted from target areas onto rubber plantations or farms, damaging trees and food crops which were not approved for destruction. Villages in reasonably secure areas were at times inexplicably targeted for crop destruction. Leaflets were dropped twenty-four hours before spraying so that peasants could evacuate their villages and farms.

Certain so called free-spraying areas were exempt from the system of formal requests and could be sprayed at any time it was considered necessary by local commanders. These areas included the demilitarized zone, the A Shau Valley on the Laotian border in the northernmost portion of South Vietnam, and the perimeters of base camps. Most helicopter missions and spraying from trucks, boats and by hand were conducted at the discretion of unit commanders. The defoliant was considered to be one of the most useful weapons at the disposal of military commanders for both tactical purposes and for denying food to the enemy.

The Viet Cong followed up spraying missions over both jungles and farms by spreading stories among the Vietnamese that the chemicals were deadly poison.

The immediately discernible results of their use were certainly frightening enough. When Agent Blue or other chemicals were applied to crops, the rice, tapioca, melons, water spinach, and other foods immediately became inedible to humans. If the food was fed to pigs or cows, the animals sickened and died.

Agent Orange was hideously destructive to the vegetation on which it was sprayed. It produced an orgy of growth so that plants literally grew themselves to death, swelling so rapidly they exploded into masses of evil-smelling vegetable matter. Leaves began to wither and rust within three to five days after spraying. Depending on the season and on the mixture of vegetation, everything growing in the jungle would be dead within one to three months after spraying. Nipa palms survived five or six weeks before they lost all their leaves and were turned into gray bloated lumps of dead vegetation. Mangrove trees were less tolerant of the poison and usually died within a week.

The jungles became as silent as graveyards. There were no sounds of insects, birds, or of larger animals after the aircraft had released their clouds of chemical. Fish in the rivers and streams floated on the surface belly-up. Vietnamese refused to enter sprayed areas. The dying jungles seemed malevolent and ghostly.

Americans, however, reassured the peasants, their own troops, and those of friendly nations that the spray was not dangerous to human or animal life. There was no evidence that anyone had ever died from exposure to the chemical, they pointed out. Enlisted men actively involved in the spraying treated the chemical so cavalierly they often worked in T-shirts or no shirts at all. At times some playfully turned the spray on each other.

Major Ralph Dresser was then in charge of the Air Force's spray missions, which had been renamed Operation Ranch Hand. Personnel attached to his unit wore green shoulder patches crossed diagonally with a brown stripe. A former all-American football player from Texas, Dresser had no fear of toxic effects from the chemical.

He was quoted in the November 1966 issue of *Flying* magazine as insisting that enemy claims that the spray was deadly poison were propaganda. Asserting to the writer of the article that he would prove that the chemical was not poison, he stuck his finger under the spigot of a dispenser drum and licked at the oily substance. "It tastes like kerosene with chemical overtones—not good, but hardly a deadly poison unless you drink it, which nobody is likely to do," he observed with practiced blandness.

Dresser's seven aircraft, an all-volunteer outfit, the Aerial Spray Flight of the 309th Aerial Commando Squadron, operated on a schedule of six days per week, two missions per day. A sign over the ready room door advised ONLY WE CAN PREVENT FORESTS.

Despite the nonchalance of professional warriors like Major Dresser, disturbing reports continued to surface. Spraying was linked to alarming increases in liver cancer, miscarriages, and deformed babies among Vietnamese and farm animals.

A spokesman for the National Liberation Front claimed in a radio broadcast from North Vietnam that the chemical was causing the deaths of newborn babies and widespread starvation. But not all the reports were coming from enemy propagandists. Even the hardy Montagnard hill people, who were such devoted allies of the Americans, had begun to show uneasiness over a possible link between spraying and the headaches, respiratory problems, and troublesome pus-filled sores they were developing. It was all rather unsettling, but the spraying operation continued. It was wartime and there was no convenient way to initiate the complex studies needed to definitely determine if the ailments and troubled births were related to the spraying.

American servicemen and their allies had little time for such worries. John Woods, like Michael Ryan, was having health problems. He was also losing weight and experiencing respiratory troubles, and his body had broken out in sores. The climate and the jungle in Vietnam seemed inherently hostile to westerners.

It was easy to attribute the health problems to Vietnam itself. Aside from possible injury in battle, illness was only one of the additional hazards of duty in Southeast Asia. The very vegetation could be formidably destructive. More than one trooper returned from patrol with his hands, arms, or legs ripped by the "wait-a-minute bush," so named because of the sharp barbs and high tensile reaction that made stumbling into it an experience akin to wrestling a pride of wildcats. It seemed to the GIs that every living thing was arrayed against them as their enemy.

The Viet Cong and North Vietnamese regulars also had effective weapons, and Michael was never more painfully aware of that than during his regiment's move from Long Binh to Xuan Loc at the foot of the Central Highlands about sixty miles northeast of Saigon.

The cavalrymen gave up their base camp at Long Binh to a newly arriving regiment, the 199th Light Infantry, and moved several miles northeast to establish a new base where they could resume operations in a heavily con- tested area infested with Viet Cong. Michael was assigned as a machine gunner and was a member of the three-man crew of an armored personnel carrier (APC) that broke down halfway through the trip. The remainder of the convoy continued on, leaving the crippled vehicle and its crew behind to fend for itself as best it could. Halting the convoy for one vehicle might invite an ambush that could lead to scores of casualties and destruction of valuable armor. The APC and its crew were left on their own in the middle of an abandoned rubber plantation. They were abandoned on a highway that was notorious for swift and savage enemy attacks.

Michael and his companions worked feverishly on the stalled APC, turning now and then to peer over their shoulders into the menacing undergrowth and rubber trees. They expected at any moment to hear the crack of rifles and the crump of exploding grenades or mortar shells. Instead, the pistons suddenly fired and the APC's engine charged back to life. The anxious trio straggled into their new base about an hour and a half after the rest of the outfit.

The perimeters of the new camp were cleared of undergrowth just as they had been at Long Binh. The larger trees were chopped down or bulldozed, and crews sprayed the remaining vegetation from trucks. The acidic, sweet odor of the spray hung in the hot humid air of Xuan Loc for days while the agonized trees, bushes, and grasses slowly turned from a healthy blue-green to a fetid, stinking gray-brown mass of swollen and twisted stalks with dropping, dying leaves.

Michael was in Xuan Loc for Thanksgiving. He had KP. It was a job he drew only four times during his Army career—both Thanksgiving holidays and both birthdays he spent in the service. He missed the turkey dinner that most other troopers shared—soldiers on KP ate after the others were through and by the time it was his turn, there was no turkey left.

A few days after Thanksgiving, he and several buddies from Brooklyn sat up together until 3 AM listening to the Armed Forces Radio Network broadcast of the Notre Dame–Michigan State football game. The Associated Press selected one team as the best college squad in the nation, and United Press International chose the other. The Brooklyn soldiers bet to a man on Notre Dame. The game ended in a ten-to-ten tie and all bets were off.

Michael had other problems to worry about besides missed turkey dinners and football games. Pressures were beginning to build on his young bride in the Bronx. No matter how busy or how exhausted he was, Michael had conscientiously written to Maureen almost every day since leaving the United States. The envelopes were addressed to "Miss Maureen O'Connor." But inside the envelopes, his letters began, "Dear Mrs. Ryan."

One of Maureen's younger sisters found some of the letters and read them. She realized that her older sister was married and threatened to tell their mother. Maureen managed to keep the lid on the secret by lending clothes to her sister and agreeing to various other favors she demanded. It wasn't an easy tightrope to walk. Maureen was frustrated, angry, and lonely, and she complained to her husband. Their parents had to be told about the marriage. "I don't care how you get home," she wrote, "but get home."

Michael was entitled to six days of R & R—rest and relaxation. At that time his furlough could be taken in Tokyo, Hong Kong, or Hawaii. He and his friend Tommy Rafferty applied for Christmas vacation in Hawaii.

The Fort deRussy military reservation along colorful Kalakaua Avenue in the heart of Waikiki has provided shelter and entertainment for servicemen and women on pass or furlough during three wars. It has one of the finest beaches in Waikiki and is reserved solely for military personnel, dependents, and their guests. Michael and his friend from Brooklyn didn't spend even an hour on the beach. They stayed at Fort deRussy barely long enough to listen to a lieutenant colonel warn them and other GIs on R & R not to leave Hawaii. "What are they gonna do, send us to Germany?" Michael asked his companion.

An hour later they were on an airplane flying to JFK International Airport in New York. Rafferty was engaged to be married and was as anxious to get home as Michael was.

Mick Ryan met his son at the airport. A few minutes after greeting the rest of the family, Michael was driving through a vicious snow storm on the way to the Bronx with his sister Patty. It was midmorning on the day before Christmas.

Patty knocked on the door of the apartment while Michael flattened himself against the wall in the hallway. A moment later, with her hair in curlers and a mop in her hand, Maureen opened the door. She didn't see Michael, and after greeting Patty, she turned to lead the way into the apartment. Michael slipped up behind her and tapped her on the shoulder.

Early Christmas morning Michael told his sister Deirdre about his marriage. Her reaction was the same as Patty's had been. She wanted to be warned before her parents were told so that she could find a safe refuge. Michael and Maureen decided to wait another day or two before telling their parents of the marriage. Then they waited another day.

His parents were finally told the day before he left home again for Hawaii and Vietnam. His father had just come home from work and his mother was expected to arrive in a few minutes with about a dozen relatives who wanted to visit with Michael. Michael, Maureen, his father, and his sisters were seated at the dining room table when he leaned over, propping his arms on his elbow, rested his chin in the palm of one hand and took a deep breath.

"Guess what, Dad?" he began. Maureen reached between them and squeezed Michael's hand with hers.

Mick Ryan's brow knotted, and he ventured a couple of guesses. Michael was going to be discharged early? He was going to return to school full-time after his Army service was completed? He was going to buy a car?

"We got married."

The elder Ryan's florid face drained of color, his cheeks

tightened, then began to fill with red. Mick and Vicky Ryan would never attend their only son's wedding. They knew, of course, that Michael and Maureen were in love, and had in fact already placed a one hundred dollar deposit on a hall for the wedding reception. But now there wouldn't be a reception. Mick Ryan thought of his wife. She would be heartbroken.

She was. Vicky Ryan walked into the house three or four minutes ahead of the relatives. Her husband broke the news. There was time only for her eyes to mist over and for her to give Maureen a quick, practiced head-to-toe inspection that was part mother-in-law, part obstetrical nurse, before the company arrived. The timing of Michael's announcement was perfect for heading off the anticipated explosion of anger and disappointment.

The next day when Mick Ryan drove his son to the airport, he asked if Maureen was pregnant.

"No," said Michael.

"Why not?" his father demanded. "You're going to give me a grandson, aren't you?"

Maureen broke the news to her mother about the marriage after returning home from the airport, where she had said a tearful goodbye to Michael. She was standing at the stove cooking dinner for Mrs. O'Connor, who had just come home from work. Maureen had her back to her mother and was so depressed about Michael's return to Vietnam she blurted out the secret.

"I want to tell you something," she said. "I'm married."

Maureen couldn't see her mother's angry eyes on her back, but she could feel them boring in.

"Are you pregnant?" Mrs. O'Connor asked.

"I don't think so," Maureen replied.

The atmosphere at the dinner table was strained that night and for several others. The impromptu wedding marked the first time that any of Mrs. O'Connor's children had seriously deceived her. And Maureen's response to the question about pregnancy hadn't eased the tension any.

Maureen continued living at home for three or four months until one day she hired a taxi and moved her clothing and other personal possessions to a cozy apartment in Brooklyn.

Michael had fourteen hours left on his R & R when his airplane touched down in Hawaii and he was depressed after ending the brief reunion with his wife. After setting aside cab fare to Fort deRussy he had barely enough money for one drink when he sat down at the bar of the Hawaii Hilton with his friend Rafferty. The bartender refused their money and paid for their drinks. When those were finished, patrons sitting on both sides of the two GIs ordered more for them. People at tables sent over still others.

When the two soldiers escaped from the bar and hailed a cab, the driver dropped them off at Fort deRussy and waved away their money. "Just take care of yourselves over there," he advised.

Michael and his friend were in Xuan Loc in time for New Year's Eve. It was one year before the bloody Tet offensive was launched. It was also seven months before Michael would see Brooklyn, his wife, and his parents and sisters again. During those seven months he concentrated on staying alive.

It wasn't an easy job to do. A few days after Michael's return to Vietnam, U.S. and South Vietnamese troops launched Operation Cedar Falls, a multidivisional sweep through the Iron Triangle, a thickly jungled Viet Cong stronghold named for its geographical shape and strong enemy troop concentration and defense.

The chief target was the Viet Cong's Fourth Military Region Headquarters, which was responsible for terrorist and other offensive operations in the Saigon area some twenty-five kilometers to the south. The Eleventh Armored Cavalry Regiment and the 173rd Airborne Brigade that John Woods was serving with were two of the major units participating in the three-week long operation. The enemy headquarters was destroyed, and tons of rice and weapons were captured. Capture of a half-million pages of documents was described by the American command as the largest intelligence breakthrough of the war up to that time.

The American and South Vietnamese incursion into the Iron Triangle was a major operation and historic battle, but one of Michael's most vivid memories of Vietnam was of the first soldier he saw die. It occurred less than a week after the full regiment arrived at Long Binh.

Michael was showering when another trooper completed bathing, toweled off, dressed, and began his walk back to his tent. A boy, ten or eleven years old, jumped up from elephant grass just outside the newly cleared perimeter and fired a single shot. The round pierced the GI's arm and went through his lungs. That night Michael had difficulty falling asleep. The dead soldier was a teenager, not much older than the boy who had shot him. Michael couldn't stop puzzling over the forces that could cause one boy to kill another boy he had never met or seen before.

The closest scrape with death that Michael endured in Vietnam occurred one night after most of his unit had charged off in pursuit of Viet Cong, leaving him behind with about one hundred other Americans to guard the camp. He was manning the switchboard in the communications center when he heard the first mortar shell explode. The enemy had circled around their pursuers and were attacking the lightly defended camp. Every round they fired scored a direct hit on a tent. Michael realized the rounds were being walked in a flurry of dusty explosions along the line of tents toward the communications center.

Just as he was running clear of the entrance to the concrete and metal hut and was mentally debating if he should take his chances with snakes and rats in a nearby slit-trench, a mortar shell exploded a few feet away from him. The concussion lifted him off his feet and slammed him backward, dropping him on his head and shoulders three or four yards away. His ears were ringing and a tiny trickle of blood was seeping from one of them when he staggered to his feet. Groggily he brushed his hands over his arms and legs. They were all intact, and there were no cuts, punctures, or chunks of shrapnel in his body. He was lucky. But his ears were ringing, and they continued to bother him for days.

The troops were shaken by the devastating mortar attack. One soldier, a husky, broad-shouldered former football player from Chicago, dug a huge pit directly under his bunk the next day. He lined the hole with armor scavenged from abandoned tanks, surrounded it with sandbags, and completed the project by adding a trap door. The one-man bomb shelter was impregnable and could take a direct hit from almost anything and still afford the occupant an excellent chance of survival.

Military intelligence indicated that the Viet Cong would return for a second attack the night after the initial mortar assault, so an air strike was called in to harrass them. Michael was again working at the switchboard, and when the bombs began exploding, the noise and concussion awakened a nervous trooper who had narrowly escaped injury the previous night. He leaped to his feet and ran straight through a wood-and-screen wall.

The attacks were well planned and remorselessly effective. A Viet Cong attack on a napalm bomb stockpile and ammunition dump at Long Binh set off such a dramatic pyrotechnical display that Michael feared for a moment that atomic weapons had been introduced into the war. Although he was more than two miles from the dump, the concussion, noise, and glare of the explosions and fire were awesome. The devastating attack was carried out by enemy sapper squads which penetrated base defenses and touched off explosive charges. They were apparently aided by saboteurs who worked in the munitions area. The explosions and fires lighted up the sky for hours.

The Regiment suffered severe losses in its clashes with the Viet Cong, but its armor and troopers made up a formidable fighting force which inflicted heavy casualties on the enemy. The Eleventh Armored Cavalry fielded more fire power than any other American ground unit in Vietnam. There were some 900 armored personnel carriers equipped with three machine guns each and about 150 tanks—each equipped with a cannon and a machine gun.

Michael didn't fire any of the awesome weaponry mounted on the armored vehicles in combat. And although he qualified as an expert marksman, he fired his M-16 automatic rifle only a few times at snipers during attacks on the base camp.

Most of his personal experiences in Vietnam were relatively prosaic compared to those of others who were regularly sent on patrols, search-and-destroy missions, or convoy escort. One of his less enviable jobs was burning excrement from the latrines. The latrines were primitively but efficiently constructed from fifty-gallon drums cut in half and placed in pits sunk under wooden boards. When the drums were full, they were pulled out and carried away so that the contents could be burned. The empty cans were then returned to their place under the boards for reuse.

The soldiers who served in Vietnam in the mid-1960s were among the last of the Elvis generation. Michael and most of his buddies thought the Beatles were long-haired freaks whose appeal would soon fade. The GIs of that period were not rebels or nonconformists. They believed in their country and in their country's policies. They were prepared, if not always happy, to sacrifice for its welfare.

Soldiers of the mid-60s nevertheless could still harbor the traditional GI resentment of officers, whose duties, naturally, did not include such offensive tasks as latrine detail. So it was that one day Michael heated one of the oil drums until it was glowing pink, then hefted it in a gloved hand and replaced it in the officer's latrine. He watched the commotion from 100 yards away a few moments later as officers fled in every direction, hoisting their trousers with one hand or buckling their belts on the run, while flames and smoke billowed from the latrine.

One of the most dangerous combat jobs in Vietnam was crewman aboard the Army's HU-1A "Huey" helicopter gunships. Michael's cousin, Donald, was true to his word and had reenlisted in the Army. He was a lean, tough, and self-assured professional soldier, and the next time he and Michael saw each other after the going away party, he was a helicopter pilot.

Michael had extended his yearlong tour of duty in the combat zone an extra twenty days in return for an early discharge, and was sweating out his last thirty days in Vietnam as a radioman. Soldiers who returned to the United States with less than ninety days to serve were released from active duty immediately instead of being assigned to new duty stations.

Like most short timers who were so close to home and safety, Michael became more determined than ever to avoid unnecessary risks. Horror stories are circulated in every war of soldiers who are killed or wounded on their last day in combat. He was determined to return home safe and whole to his wife.

Michael was asleep in his bunk when another soldier shook him awake and said that an officer was looking for him. It was Donald, and he was the pilot of one of a half-dozen Hueys which had just landed at the camp. Donald wanted his cousin to help him arrange for breakfast for the helicopter crews.

The helicopters were assigned to a series of strafing missions in the area that day, and the cooks readily agreed to provide the breakfasts. They also suggested that the crews return for the noon meal of hamburgers and french fries. About midmorning five of the aircraft returned to the base and the crews were served coffee. The sixth helicopter had been shot down. When Donald led his flight back to the base for lunch, only four helicopters were left. All four returned to the base after an afternoon mission, but one of them crashed on the runway. In less than eight hours the helicopters and crews had absorbed a fifty-percent casualty rate.

Michael was waiting at the air field when his cousin landed, and Donald explained that he needed help once more. The pressure on his door gunner was so intense the soldier was not emotionally capable of handling his duties on the next mission, Donald explained. It was understandable that the man had cracked. Gunners were strapped into the doorways of their helicopters and stood on two steel rods while directing a stream of fire at their objectives. They were natural targets. Donald said he knew Michael was an excellent marksman and he wanted him to fill in for the ailing gunner.

"I'm not going," Michael quickly replied. His respected older cousin suddenly appeared in a new perspective. Donald was an officer—the traditional tormentor of enlisted men. All the stories Michael had heard of hapless short timers injured or killed rushed back into his head.

Donald was angry. He finally appealed to a major. "This man is my cousin. He's a good marksman, and I want him as my gunner," he told the senior officer.

"You're the new gunner, son," the major said, nodding his head at Michael.

Michael tightened his jaw, and his brows bunched, narrowing his eyes into stubborn slits. "I'm not going."

"That's an order," the major replied. Donald watched silently, his mouth pulled into a grim line as he stared unblinking at his cousin.

"No way," Michael repeated. "I've only got three weeks left in this place, and I'm not getting my ass shot off now for anything!"

Donald and the major burst out laughing. A half hour later Donald lifted off in his helicopter for the last time that day, accompanied by his own gunner. The confrontation had been staged. It was an example of Donald's raucous humor. Although the flap about drafting Michael into his crew was a joke, nevertheless Donald later admitted he would have taken his cousin on the flight if he had agreed to go.

Michael was marking off his last few days in Vietnam when Rafferty rushed up to him one night and said he had to borrow some money. Rafferty was from St. Thomas Aquinas parish, about five blocks from Michael's home, and they had become close friends. The situation had changed from the days of their childhood when the mere fact that they were from different parishes would have been cause enough for an immediate fist fight.

Rafferty had lost about $1,000 shooting craps with a

soldier from Chicago and needed a loan to get back in the game. He was a skillful gambler with cards and dice, and Michael had loaned him money before. He usually repaid the loans double.

Although Michael always sent all but a few dollars of his monthly pay home to his wife and his mother, it was only a day or two after payday and he had $300. Rafferty took it all. When the gambler rushed off to another tent to get back in the game, Michael went with him. Rafferty's luck hadn't changed. He was rolling snake eyes, and the soldier from Chicago was throwing passes and making points. Rafferty was down to his last $10 when he got hot. Letting the money ride, he threw one point after another until he had won Michael's money back, recovered his own money, and cleaned out the other soldier. When the two friends from Brooklyn walked out of the tent, Rafferty peeled off almost $600 from his roll of bills and gave it to Michael.

Michael boarded an airplane for his flight to the United States a few days later. He was a Specialist Four, with almost $600 in his pocket. Mustering-out pay would swell the bankroll to more than $1,000 by the time he loaded his barracks bag aboard a bus and left the Army processing center near San Francisco as a civilian. He had slashed eighty-nine days from his previous discharge date. The twenty-day gamble in Vietnam had paid off. Now he could begin a new life in the real world.

4

WAITING FOR
KERRY

Everything was new in the home Maureen had selected
for her and her husband in a predominantly Italian neighborhood of Brooklyn known as Mill Basin. She located a
snug, one-bedroom apartment on the ground floor of a
newly constructed house owned by a New York City policeman. The policeman lived upstairs.

New furniture was selected, the refrigerator was
stocked with food, and she had put together a new ward-
robe for Michael. But the combined pay of a receptionist
and an Army Spec Four was stretched to its limit by ex-
penditures. She apologized to her husband that there was
no money left over for a honeymoon.

That was when Michael revealed his own surprise. He
pulled the $1,000 he had accumulated during his last few
days in the Army from a money belt under his shirt and
dropped the bills on a table. The Ryans honeymooned in
Virginia Beach.

Following the honeymoon they resumed their jobs at
IBM. Michael moved from the mailroom to a job as a
computer trainee, and Maureen continued working as a
receptionist. The war in Vietnam quickly began to fade

from their consciousness and was relegated to an event that they watched fleetingly on the nightly television news.

The Ryans focused their attention on their home, their work, and their lives together. Michael registered again at St. John's University. He also indulged in some serious eating. In Vietnam, when he hadn't been thinking of Maureen, he was daydreaming about vanilla malteds, roast beef, and hero sandwiches. Almost as quickly as his weight had dropped in Vietnam, it began to balloon after his return home. He had never weighed more than 178 pounds, but during his first year home, his waistline swelled from 27 inches to 41 inches, and his weight rose to 215 pounds.

Beer wasn't a factor in the added weight. He had some-how lost his previous ability to swallow great quantities of beer without getting drunk, and even the most moderate drinking caused him to slur his speech, and walk un-steadily, and left him hung over for two days. The mere odor of alcohol was enough to bring on a migraine head-ache, which had been bothering him since his days in Vietnam. He learned to swallow aspirin by the handful without lessening pain that was so severe it made him nauseous.

Since returning home he was also bothered with nerv-ousness, which he assumed would improve as he adjusted to civilian life. But his most aggravating health problem was the rash that had plagued him sporadically since his first weeks in Long Binh. Angry red lumps and pus-filled sores erupted again and speckled the insides of his legs and thighs. Lesser outbreaks covered his back and but-tocks, while other unsightly lumps and blackheads devel-oped on his neck and behind his ears.

Michael speculated to his mother that he had jungle rot. She took one look at the sores and shook her head.

"Don't tell me that's jungle rot," she corrected him. "Your father got jungle rot when he was in New Guinea, and this stuff isn't the same thing."

The condition was uncomfortable and embarrassing. If Michael stretched his legs too far when he was walking, the skin sometimes pulled too tight and the sores ruptured. Blood trickled down his legs and the pus stuck to his clothing.

Another reminder of his service in Vietnam was an almost constant ringing in his ears. Eventually he made an appointment with his family doctor for an examination. The physician solemnly peered into one ear with a tiny flashlight, then without a word walked behind his patient and probed the other ear. A few moments later he replaced the light in his shirt pocket. His eyebrows squeezed into a frown.

"One of your eardrums is gone, and the other is just about shot," he advised. "What happened to you in the Army?"

Michael was startled. "Nothing," he said. "I never got hit or anything like that."

"Well, you weren't drafted that way," the physician observed. "They would never have taken you."

Michael realized that he hadn't really escaped the near hit from the mortar blast as cleanly as he had previously believed. His ears had been ringing when he picked himself off the ground after the explosion, and they had hardly stopped buzzing since then.

Armed with the physician's diagnosis, Michael applied to the Veterans Administration for disability benefits. He was given a physical examination, and VA physicians compared his medical history with records of his military service before approving a ten-percent disability claim based on the damaged eardrums, migraine headaches, and a nervous condition.

Despite his health problems life was generally good to Michael. He began getting acquainted with Maureen's younger brothers, who stayed with them during summer vacations. After the first couple of years, the two older boys visited less often, but the youngest, Brian, returned every summer as well as during extended vacations from classes such as the Christmas and Easter holidays. Gradually Brian became a permanent member of the household, and Michael developed an extremely close emotional bond with him that somewhat resembled a father-son relationship. But Brian also became the brother that Michael never had.

Although they were raised as Roman Catholics and looked forward to rearing a family, the couple decided to postpone parenthood until they had acquired their own home and accumulated a modest bank account. As a teenager from a large family of responsible and loving brothers and sisters, Maureen entered marriage assuming she would rear a houseful of children. But she began to seriously consider family planning after Michael mailed her a book he read in Vietnam which dealt with the subject.

Despite the Church's restrictions on popular forms of birth control, they decided—like many modern Catholics —that the practice was in their own best interests. It was a matter between themselves and God. There would be time for children who were planned, prepared for, and wanted. In the meantime Michael and Maureen saved every dollar they could, putting the money aside to be used as a down payment on a house.

A few miles from the Ryans, John Woods was also readjusting to life as a civilian with his wife, Mildred, and two daughters. He had obtained a full-time job as a city bus driver and occupied most of his weekends working as a wardmaster in a Veterans' Administration Hospital.

Like Michael Ryan, John Woods had been plagued with health problems since his return from Vietnam. He, too, had trouble with nerves, and he continued to experience vexatious skin eruptions that first surfaced while he was stationed near Long Binh. There were also times when he was inexplicably doubled over with disabling stomach cramps, and he began to experience chest pains which were so piercingly distressing he broke into cold sweats. Doctors to whom he described the symptoms examined him and shook their heads. The chest pains were false heart attacks, they said. Woods began to worry that the doctors thought he was a hypochondriac.

Mildred Woods was also experiencing new problems relating to her health and the way her body functioned. Although she had experienced two normal and successful pregnancies prior to her husband's second tour in Vietnam, she miscarried twice after his return. Two other pregnancies resulted in the birth of sons. One of the boys was born with a large benign tumor of the lymph gland on his face. Six operations failed to totally correct his disfigurement. The other son developed high blood pressure and disabling muscle spasms.

Halfway across the world, the United States continued to pour troops and equipment into the war in Southeast Asia. In January 1968, six months after Michael left the war zone, Communist forces attacked Saigon and some thirty provincial capitals and government strongholds during Tet, the Vietnamese New Year. They were beaten back with damaging losses, but American news accounts created an impression that the Tet Offensive was a great victory for the Communists, rather than a defeat. Some four months later, peace talks opened in Paris.

Paul Reutershan was a seventeen-year-old redhead from Mohegan Lake in Westchester County, N.Y., when the first faltering moves toward peace were initiated in Paris. He was a recent high-school graduate and had enlisted in the Army to learn a trade, so that he could obtain a good-paying job after returning to civilian life.

After basic and advanced training he was given flight courses, including instruction in aircraft mechanics, and was sent to Vietnam, where he was stationed at Bien-Hoa as a crew chief on a helicopter.

Reutershan and his crew transported supplies to the Army's 20th Engineering Brigade, which was occupied clearing cover from jungle areas likely to be used by Communist guerrillas or North Vietnamese. Reutershan's helicopter regularly followed close behind the slow-moving C-123s of Operation Ranch Hand. Almost daily they flew through the white jets of herbicide billowing from the bellies of the larger aircraft. The helicopter crewmen knew the spray was an herbicide, but they had been told it was harmless to humans.

As Reutershan was flying missions in April 1969, American troop strength in Vietnam peaked at 543,400 men. It was the same month that Robert "Bobby" Muller, a twenty three-year-old Marine lieutenant from California, was wounded. He stood to lead his squad up a hill near Con Thien when he was struck by a bullet that crashed through his chest, collapsed his lungs, and severed his spinal cord. The injuries left him permanently paralyzed below midchest.

President Lyndon B. Johnson chose not to seek reelection in 1968, and less than three months after American troop strength reached its zenith in Vietnam, Richard M. Nixon, the new President, began gradual withdrawal of U.S. forces in accordance with a new policy of Victnamization of the war. Vietnamization called for greater dependence on South Vietnam's domestic manpower and military. A strong American presence nevertheless continued to be necessary—and costly. Every week the bodies of young soldiers were returned to lie in cemeteries in cities and towns across America, and hundreds of others like Bobby Mueller entered VA hospitals for treatment and repair of the terrible injuries they suffered in the undeclared war.

A North Vietnamese scientist, Dr. Ton That Tung, began addressing the world press and lecturing at scientific gatherings, warning that Agent Orange and related herbicides were causing severe health problems and birth defects among humans and animals. The chemical appeared to be linked to the development of chloracne, a chronic and vexing rash, and to sustained vomiting, as well as to birth defects and miscarriages that were increasingly showing up among Vietnamese. Ironically, although it was Dr. Tung's treatment of North Vietnamese soldiers returning from combat areas that had led to his conclusions about the chemical causing cancer, he was prevented from publicizing complete information because his government was still insisting it had no troops in the South.

Dr. Tung's warnings were dismissed by most American authorities as propaganda. Dr. Tung was, after all, Vice Minister of Health for North Vietnam and the former personal physician to Ho Chi Minh. Sensational stories in

Saigon newspapers claiming that the chemicals were pro-
voking an epidemic of miscarriages and deformed babies
were also largely ignored. But developments in the
United States as the 1960s drew to a close and the 1970s
dawned forced Congress to take note of the warnings.

The Bionetics Research Laboratories in Bethesda,
Maryland, had been commissioned in 1964 by the National Institutes of Health's National Cancer Institute to
test various popularly used pesticides and industrial substances for carcinogenic (cancer causing) and teratogenic
(fetus deforming) effects on laboratory animals.

2,4,5-T and 2,4-D, the chemicals used in Agent Orange,
had been in government and civilian use in this country
for more than two decades and were routinely applied to
thousands of acres of crops, rangeland, timber, and lawns.
In various forms the chemicals and their close cousins had
been used for defoliation and herbicidal spraying of crops
in Southeast Asia for nearly three years. Yet the series of
studies commissioned to the Bionetics Laboratory, ordered only after mounting pressure from biologists and
other concerned environmentalists, apparently marked
the first time the possible teratogenic properties of the
compounds were ever submitted to serious scientific scru-
tiny by a government agency or manufacturer.

Several months after experiments began, the secret
study had disclosed that 2,4,5-T in small doses caused
birth defects in rats and mice.

Information in the preliminary report on 2,4,5-T was
initially made available only to a handful of officials in the
Department of Defense and the Department of Agriculture. Results of the study were forwarded to the Food and
Drug Administration and, of course, the National Cancer
Institute. In 1969, when the NCI finally released information gleaned from the study to the public, only carcinogenic findings were disclosed. Information about the

fetus-deforming properties of 2,4,5-T was not published.

A few months later an angry FDA employee leaked the remaining information to an investigator for consumer advocate Ralph Nader. The investigator was reportedly told that the full report was not publicized because it was feared the information would fuel the antiwar movement and draw international criticism accusing the United States of waging chemical warfare.

True to prediction, as soon as the full report was publicly disclosed, protests began on college campuses, and criticism mounted in Congress. The chemical industry fought back. Dow Chemical Corporation, one of the nation's largest producers of chemicals, charged that the sample of 2,4,5-T used by Bionetics was heavily contaminated with an impurity created during the manufacturing process. The impurity, normally present in the herbicide only in trace quantities, was 2,3,7,8-tetrachloro-dibenzo-para-dioxin, commonly known as dioxin or as TCDD.

A continuing round of studies eventually confirmed that the dangerous fetus-deforming agent was not 2,4,5-T, but its contaminant, dioxin. Dioxin has been found to be so toxic that only the most minuscule amounts, a few hundred parts per trillion, can kill animals and cripple their young. It is so virulent that three ounces poured into the water supply of New York City would be enough to kill the entire population. The deadly by-product was eventually labeled by scientists as perhaps the most toxic small molecule and teratogenic chemical compound known to man.

On October 29, 1969, Dr. Lee Du Bridge, science advisor to President Nixon, announced a series of actions aimed at softening the mounting domestic criticism of the defoliation program. The most significant act appeared to be a decision to restrict the use of 2,4,5-T in Vietnam to remote areas away from populated areas, as well as curtailing its domestic use on most food crops and banning government spray programs in populated areas by January 1, 1970. Du Bridge conceded that the act was prompted by information disclosed by the Bionetics study indicating a possible link between the chemical and a high percentage of stillbirths and malformations among fetuses in laboratory animals.

Any elation that antispray forces may have felt at the announcement was tempered the next day when Department of Defense spokesmen indicated that their policy in Vietnam already conformed to the presidential directive!

Opposition to spraying continued to mount as a political issue, and in March 1970 the Pentagon announced a twenty-five-percent reduction in the spraying program in Vietnam. On April 15, U.S. Senator Philip Hart of Michigan presided at a hearing by a subcommittee on Energy, the Environment, and Natural Resources to further probe the controversial forest-defoliation and crop-destruction operations in Southeast Asia. Testimony from biologists confirmed the original conclusions of the Bionetics study and indicated grave danger to human and animal fetuses.

Senator Hart responded by warning that 2,4,5-T might unleash "the most horrible tragedy ever known to mankind." Even the U.S. Surgeon General cautioned that the chemical might be hazardous to "women of childbearing age."

The Department of Defense was forced to act. It announced that "pending review," the spraying of 2,4,5-T in Vietnam would be halted. The announcement did not affect 2,4-D, the companion ingredient used to manufacture Agent Orange. Consequently spraying of Agent White, the other defoliant containing 2,4-D, was not blocked. Agent White was produced by mixing 2,4-D with picloram, an herbicide with such long-term efficacy that its use was not permitted on crops in the United States.

A General Accounting Office report later disclosed that the last herbicidal spraying mission by a fixed-wing aircraft over South Vietnam occurred on January 7, 1971. The last helicopter spraying operation "under United States control" was flown on October 31, 1971.

Prior to cessation of Agent Orange–spraying missions, from 10.5 to 12 million gallons of the defoliant and its predecessor, Agent Purple, had been applied in Southeast Asia to five million acres of jungle and cropland, an area about the size of the state of Connecticut. The concentration of 2,4,5-T in Agent Orange applied to the foliage in Vietnam averaged thirteen times that of the chemical used in the United States. On some missions entire loads of the chemical were jettisoned all at once when the aircraft was attacked or equipment problems developed.

Although its decision to halt the use of Agent Orange in Vietnam was a tacit admission by the Department of Defense that the chemical was potentially dangerous to humans and their offspring, no effort was made by government agencies to notify exposed servicemen and veterans of the suspicions. No one notified Michael Ryan, John Woods, or Paul Reutershan.

Reutershan survived his tour in Vietnam, and when he returned home, it was to a nation swept by antiwar demonstrations. Two weeks after the spraying was halted, President Nixon announced that American and South Vietnamese troops had crossed the Cambodian border to raid Communist supply centers and outposts used for staging enemy attacks. Demonstrations occurred on city streets and college campuses. On May 4, 1970, after three days of student upheavals, arson and vandalism at Kent State University in Ohio, more than 2,000 demonstrators collected on the Commons, a seven-acre grassy area on the campus. Tear gas was used in an effort to force the crowd to disperse, but when the demonstrators began lobbing the gas cannisters back at the troop formation, the guardsmen suddenly fired their rifles into the massed crowd. When the shooting halted twenty-six seconds later, thirteen students had been hit. Four of them were dead.

Veterans returning home during the glut of national guilt and uncertainty were treated like pariahs. Reutershan and his contemporaries had to reintegrate into a society plagued with uneasiness or outright opposition to the war they had been fighting. To many, especially some young Americans, the draft resisters who had fled to other countries to escape their military obligation were the real heroes of the war.

The veterans were either ignored or branded as psychos or junkies—blood brothers to the notorious Lt. William Calley, who shared responsibility for the massacre of scores of helpless Vietnamese civilians in My Lai. Newspapers and television news programs carried stories almost daily of an epidemic of heroin use among American soldiers in Vietnam, and of GIs who murdered unpopular officers. It was not popular to point out that most returning veterans were good citizens who were mentally stable and productive—or potentially productive members of society.

To be productive, of course, they needed jobs. And there were not many jobs waiting for veterans. The air industries were laying off mechanics instead of hiring them when Reutershan returned home. It wasn't long before he began answering newspaper ads and pounding on doors looking for a job. Any job.

At about the time Reutershan was desperately seeking civilian employment, Michael Ryan was tiring of his job.

He didn't want to spend his life working with machines; he wanted to work directly with people. He decided to become a policeman. Police work would provide him a practical opportunity to fulfill his desire to be of service to others, he reasoned. And the job would not be boring.

Michael and Maureen decided that he should apply for a job with the Suffolk County Police Department, from which his uncle had recently retired. The next examination for the department wasn't scheduled until February, more than six months in the future. In the meantime Michael took the written examination for the New York City Police Department. He reasoned that it would provide a good warm-up for the Suffolk County test. He got a perfect score. With veterans' credits, his mark was 109.9, tying him with fifteen other applicants.

Buoyed by his performance with the written and physical examinations, he changed his plans and decided to accept a position with the city. It came as a total shock when he was advised that he didn't qualify for the job because he had failed the physical examination. "We don't take disabled veterans," he was told.

Michael couldn't believe what he was hearing. He was stunned. "What do you mean, disabled veteran?" he demanded.

The policeman glanced at a sheaf of papers on his desk, then shifted his expressionless eyes back to the applicant. "You're getting disability from the Veterans Administration, aren't you? It says so right here on the application."

Michael went to the VA. "I don't have migraine headaches anymore," he said. "I'm not nervous, and I can hear fine."

The VA accepted his word that he was cured and agreed to remove him from their disability lists and stop his checks. There was no fuss, no physical examination.

He returned to the Police Academy. "I'm not disabled anymore," he said. "I've taken care of everything."

A week later he began training at the Academy.

As soon as the physical training instructors at the Police Academy saw how easily Michael moved his bulk through water, they assigned him to teach other recruits to swim. Surrounded by active young men who were in good physical condition, Michael began to use the pool and gymnasium to get his body back into shape. He drastically cut his food intake. He did calisthenics four hours a day, swam the length of the academy pool several times, and jogged.

Immediately after graduation from the Academy, Michael was assigned to a foot post in the 71st precinct, along the Eastern Parkway in the Crown Heights section of Brooklyn. It was his job to guard a Hasidic temple and community center.

The area he patrolled was tense. After suffering through various assaults, rapes, and robberies, some of the Jewish residents organized a vigilante group to patrol the area and to fight if necessary. By the time Michael began his assignment, militant whites were riding around shooting at blacks who ventured into the neighborhood, and militant blacks were reported to be riding in other cars shooting at Jews. Policemen were cast in the unfortunate role of enemy, referee, and innocent bystander. Many of the blacks were militantly anti-white, and especially hated police. Four officers were ambushed on the post before Michael was assigned there. His nights on the street in the 71st precinct were as coldly menacing and dangerous as the nights he had spent in Vietnam.

Other crises proved equally nerve-racking, if less dangerous, for a police officer. It is not unknown for a rookie policeman to be faced with the necessity of helping deliver a baby, and Michael was sharing a patrol car with an older, more experienced officer when they were sent to a fifth-floor walk-up where a young black woman was about to give birth. Filled with a rookie's eagerness and passion for his new job, Michael led the way, excitedly pounding up the stairs as his more phlegmatic partner followed at a leisurely pace.

The tenement apartment was full of people. Parents, aunts, uncles, brothers and sisters of the mother-to-be were crowded into the shabby kitchen and bedroom. The young woman was on the bed moaning and clutching helplessly at her swollen stomach. Her mother was screaming and cursing at her because she was unmarried and bringing disgrace to the family. The older policeman peered with mild interest through a doorway at the woman lying on the bed, then turned to Michael.

"Did you ever deliver a baby, kid?"

"No, I never did, and I don't especially want to," said Michael.

"It's yours," the veteran proclaimed with an air of bored authority. With that settled, the veteran cop ambled into the narrow kitchen, sat down at a table, and sipped at the tepid cup of black coffee he had poured for himself.

The partners weren't carrying radios, so Michael clattered downstairs to their squad car and radioed for an ambulance. Then he headed back up the stairs, vaulting past the peeling, graffiti-covered walls two steps at a time. Somehow he helped the mother deliver the baby, cut the umbilical cord, and was hovering solicitously over her when the ambulance arrived. Other members of the family remained in the room and watched throughout the ordeal, but no one offered to help.

Michael handed the infant to the mother moments before she and her son were carried downstairs in a stretcher to the waiting ambulance. He was relieved, but he also felt a mixture of awe and pride when he realized that it would not be many months before he would be holding a child of his own. Both he and Maureen now had good jobs, and they had decided it was time to start their family.

The weight-loss regimen had continued, and even though he had left the Police Academy, Michael remained devoted to a regular schedule of calisthenics. Almost every day he loped around Marine Park in Brooklyn. The fat melted away, and he dropped from a bulging 215-pounder who couldn't do a single chin up to a lean and sinewy 165-pounder who could do fifty. He stopped smoking and, except for the sores on his legs, which had erupted again after disappearing for a while, he felt healthier than he had in almost four years.

Maureen's weight hadn't varied more than a few ounces since she graduated from high school. She kept in shape doing calisthenics and, when she had the opportunity, by swimming. She and Michael appeared to be in excellent health when their child was conceived.

As soon as Michael's mother learned of the pregnancy, she selected the obstetrician and established a special diet for her daughter-in-law. Maureen continued her calisthenics and began practicing hatha yoga and deep-breathing exercises. She supplemented their diet with vitamin pills, reasoning that a healthy mother and father would produce a healthy baby.

Michael and Maureen had decided that he would take the examination for the Suffolk County Police Department and change jobs. His parents had also decided that their future lay on Long Island, and they purchased a huge four-bedroom home in Kings Park. "One of these days we're going to fill all these rooms with grandchildren," Vicky Ryan told her brood. But in the meantime, and until the parents' retirement, it was decided that Michael and Maureen would live there.

Michael had begun to have second thoughts about his chances of living to see his children grow up. Armed robbery, muggings, rape, murder, and various other forms of mayhem were commonplace in his precinct. There was no indication that the friction between the vigilantes and the blacks was letting up, and the violence was taking its toll on policemen in the form of injuries, ulcers, and broken marriages.

The sound of gunfire was familiar to officers in the 71st precinct, and Michael and his partner weren't surprised, two nights before he was scheduled to leave the New York City Police Department, when they heard the sound of rifle shots. Their orders called for them to patrol on foot, but the two uniformed policemen agreed that the neighborhood was too dangerous. They were anticipating an ambush and they had climbed into a car and prepared to ride out their patrol. The driver made a U-turn and drove in the direction of the gunshots. Two more shots were fired, and they turned again. Then two more shots were heard, apparently originating behind a school building. The officers turned their car, pulled to a stop in front of the school, and stepped out. Cautiously they began to creep around the building.

The next shots they heard were aimed at them. Two slugs smashed into the cement between Michael and his partner. They retreated to their car and radioed for help. Within minutes the school was surrounded. Some of the first officers who responded heard footsteps clattering down a fire escape. The sniper, or snipers, had safely made their getaway.

Michael's experience with the Suffolk County police examination had been a repeat of his performance in New York City: he received the top score. But this time he was in excellent physical condition. He was lean and muscular, and when he was asked to do chinups, he did ten fast ones without working up a sweat. He was accepted as a rookie and entered the Police Academy.

The Suffolk County Police Department, serving more than a million Long Island residents, is one of the largest police agencies in the United States, and one of the most professional. It is composed of some 2,800 men and women who are among the nation's highest paid law enforcement officers. There are patrolmen in the department who have law degrees and have been admitted to the New York bar, graduates of West Point and Annapolis, and officers with master's degrees in fields as various as English and social work.

Maureen's pregnancy was almost full term, and the baby was expected at any time when her husband graduated from the Academy. The ceremony was Friday night, and many friends and relatives watched as the rookies were officially recognized for completing their introductory police training.

Walking to his car in the parking lot following the ceremony, Michael felt overwhelmed with happiness. He was married to the woman beside him, and he loved her as deeply and passionately as he had on the day of his wedding four years earlier. He had a job that promised to be both challenging and rewarding, and the birth of his first child was no more than a few days away. Just before opening the door of the car and sliding into the passenger seat, he turned, smiled at his father, and bragged, "Well, Dad, now I've really got it made."

There is an old Irish superstition that it is bad luck to brag about one's good fortune. Somewhere, sometime, Michael had heard about the belief. But he didn't think about it that night. His life was too full and he was too happy.

His schedule allowed him Saturday free, as well as all day Sunday, until midnight when he was slated to begin his first regular shift of duty as a Suffolk County policeman. But Michael never reported for roll call on his first night of duty.

Maureen went into labor late Saturday night, and on Sunday evening Kerry was born. That night Michael took his first sick day on his new job.

The lives of Michael and Maureen Ryan would never be the same.

5

KERRY

Maureen was desperate. Kerry's head wouldn't stay in the box, and the dirt kept trickling away. Tears streaked Maureen's cheeks as she struggled to shovel more dirt into the collapsing hole, trying to avoid the pleading blue eyes of her daughter. If only Michael would understand and help. Kerry's head was still exposed, and craning desperately forward on the frail neck. It was only the body that was damaged. But Michael would have nothing to do with the task.

Kerry Ryan underwent three major surgical procedures during her first twenty-four hours of life. She somehow survived her precarious first few hours and was returned to the intensive care nursery, or neonatology unit, at Maimonides Hospital, to heal and to await a new round of examinations. Later, when she was larger and stronger, a rectum would be fashioned and attached to the opening of her colon, and her colostomy would be closed.

Still further in the future was what doctors assured the parents would be a simple operation to correct an improperly formed ureter—the tube which carries urine from the kidney to the bladder for emptying—and ortho- pedic surgery to reconstruct her malformed right arm and hand. The radius bone was absent from her forearm, and her hand was attached at what should have been the elbow. Her thumb was missing, and the fingers were con- tracted.

In her hospital bed several miles away, Kerry's mother was awake. She had refused the sleeping medication a night nurse brought her. Maureen wouldn't sleep until she knew her baby was out of surgery, and she had a report on Kerry's condition. Lying quietly in the dark- ened private room, she pressed a hand experimentally to her flattened stomach—it felt strangely soft and flaccid— as she struggled to reassemble the image of her baby in her mind.

Kerry had black hair. Somehow Maureen had never expected her baby's hair to be black. Red or blonde, per- haps, but not black. She was beautiful. Maternal pride and affection swept over the young woman. And fear! There was no way to prepare a new mother to suddenly become the parent of a critically ill, possibly dying, baby. But regardless of what was ahead, Maureen knew that she and Michael would fight alongside Kerry in her struggle for life.

Maureen's thoughts were interrupted. A nurse told her that Michael was waiting to talk to her on the telephone. Maureen slid her legs off the bed and felt around on the chilly floor with her feet, searching for her slippers. Pull- ing a robe around herself, she shuffled over to the tele- phone.

"Michael, how is she?" Maureen whispered, making no effort to hide the apprehension in her voice.

"She's out of danger and holding her own," Michael said. "We'll know more tomorrow."

When Maureen slid back under the sheets, the bed felt good and comforting. She realized that she was very tired. Drowsily she murmured a prayer for Kerry. And before finally drifting to sleep, she cried.

Kerry was three days old when her grandmother's fears about a serious heart defect were confirmed, just as the fears of intestinal imperfections had been confirmed earlier. The baby did not have a simple functional heart murmur. There was a tear in the septum, the area between the heart's chambers. Immediately after diagnosis, Kerry was given a drug to slow her heartbeat. The medication would continue to be administered until months, or years, later when she was strong enough to undergo open-heart surgery.

But for now open-heart surgery, like reconstructive surgery on her hand and arm, would have to wait. Her hand and her arm, weakened by the absence of the radial bone, were placed in a temporary cast. The immediate concern of the team of pediatricians and surgeons working to help Kerry was keeping her alive from day to day.

Each day seemed to bring with it a new crisis that increased the threat to the helpless baby clinging so precariously to life. Her family was riding an emotional roller coaster. Her mother was released from Community Hospital when Kerry was five days old. The same afternoon that she was discharged, Maureen went to Maimonides to see her daughter.

It was the first time in nearly a week that Maureen had worn anything besides a nightgown and slippers, and she felt strangely skinny and vulnerable in her unfamiliar blue jeans and sneakers. She was nervous, and curious to know if she would feel the same strong emotions when she saw Kerry again as she had the first and only time she had held her. Apprehension always made her feel cold, and she was chilled as she stepped from the elevator and walked around the corner of the hallway to the nursery.

She had asked her husband and mother-in-law not to tell her which of the babies was hers. She was certain that a mother would be able to pick out her own child. Continuing past the healthy babies, she stopped in front of the nursery glass shielding the infants who were ill or life threatened. Admitted by the nurse, the trio padded softly inside the unit. Maureen peered at the babies, trying to identify her own. She couldn't find Kerry. Frustrated, she finally gave up and turned helplessly to Michael.

He smiled and walked to an incubator in front of the nurses' station. Maureen peered at the baby inside and beamed. The child was exquisite. It was all she could do to keep from reaching inside the incubator and touching Kerry's soft dark hair. She marveled at the baby and considered the tiny bent arm. It, too, was beautiful, because it was part of Kerry. Maureen was pleased and proud of the little being that she and Michael had joined to create.

Maureen's days quickly acquired a routine that linked her closely to the hospital and to Kerry. Each morning, she would make an early phone call to check on her daughter's condition. At 11 AM Kerry's pediatrician would call the Ryan home in Brooklyn to give Maureen a more detailed report of Kerry's condition, the medical procedures that were being carried out that day, and to answer Maureen's questions. Later, Maureen searched through Vicky's medical books for information about Kerry's birth defects and asked her mother-in-law questions that afternoon or night about anything she didn't understand. At 4 PM, Maureen, Michael, and Vicky drove to the hospital in their Volkswagen to see Kerry. They often stood for hours outside the glassed-in unit, watching to see if she was breathing easily or showing signs of distress. Later, at home, Michael and Maureen would lie in bed holding each other, sharing their strength, and talking of Kerry's fight for life.

Because of the constant trips to the hospital, Michael and Maureen were staying in his sister Patty's former room at his parents' house in Brooklyn. Patty had married a Vietnam veteran, and obtained a job as a nurse at the Kings Park Psychiatric Hospital. Michael drove the 140-mile round trip to and from work in Suffolk County each day or evening. Maureen had taken a leave-of-absence from her job at IBM.

The miles on the battered Volkswagen accumulated rapidly as Michael steered it between the hospital, his parents' home in Brooklyn where he and his wife were staying, and Suffolk County. During the first weeks after Kerry's birth, he stopped at his own home only to pick up fresh clothing or mail. His first days as a rookie with the Suffolk County Police Department passed in a confused haze. Yet he somehow managed to function acceptably, and carried out his duties. The routine continued for months before Michael and Maureen returned to their home on Long Island. Kerry was still in the hospital.

One day, when the desire to see Kerry was overwhelming, Maureen left the house early and rode a train to the hospital. She stood alone, peering through the glass window. About three-quarters of Kerry's dark baby hair had been shaved to accommodate IVs. She was naked in the incubator, except for a diaper.

A hand was placed gently on Maureen's shoulder, startling her. She looked up into the face of a nurse who smiled and asked if she would like to go inside and hold Kerry. Maureen donned a mask and green surgical gown and walked among a sea of incubators. The nurse opened a glass bubble above Kerry and lifted the child out, transferring her to Maureen's arms.

A lump formed in Maureen's throat and tears squeezed from her eyes, trickling down to wet the mask. As she peered down at her baby, the exposed colostomy began to expel feces onto Kerry's stomach, and blood seeped through the membrane. Maureen didn't worry about the missing hair, the damaged arm or hand after that. Kerry was in a desperate battle for her life.

Maureen spent days and nights with her sick baby before doctors were able to assure her that Kerry had once again passed a crisis. She dragged herself home to meet Michael when he returned from work. They were mentally, emotionally, and physically exhausted, but that was forgotten as they rejoiced and thanked God their daughter was alive.

A few hours later the telephone rang and someone at the hospital advised them that Kerry's condition had suddenly worsened—she wasn't expected to live through the night. They called Michael's parents to tell them about Kerry, and a few minutes later the Volkswagen was backing out of the driveway and racing toward the city.

Peering helplessly through the windows at the incubator and the tortured baby inside, Kerry's family was appalled by her condition. Her delicate skin had been punctured, probed, and slashed since her first hour of life. It was covered with wounds inflicted by teams of pediatricians and surgeons intent on buying time for the baby until it was possible to correct nature's most serious mistakes. Tubes sprouted from her nose and from her frail arms like plastic plants in a hothouse jungle of electronic monitors and life-support machines. A green scapular hung from the tiny incubator, placed there by her Grandmother Ryan as a prayer and token of devotion to the Madonna.

The mothers and other relatives of healthy babies in the nursery sometimes stepped a few feet away to stare through the window at the infants in the neonatology unit. Michael's mother was standing nearby like a silent sentinel one day when two women walked over to peer through the glass at the sick babies.

"Oh, look at that," one of the women gasped to her companion, pointing to Kerry. "Look at the baby with the tiny arm."

Victoria Ryan's body stiffened and her shoulders hunched as if she were bracing herself against a chill wind. She gritted her teeth. A single startled glance at her eyes was all it took to put the women to flight. They walked hurriedly down the hall.

Kerry's grandmother and pediatrician had marshaled a formidible team of medical professionals to assist her in her struggle for survival. Nonetheless, there seemed to be no end to the string of disappointments and emergencies. X-rays disclosed that Kerry's sacrum, the lower portion of her spine, was underdeveloped. It was quite possible, doctors advised, that she would never walk.

It seemed that every time she began to gather strength and the Ryans' lives were about to return to some degree of normality, another operation or test was performed and another defect discovered. When Michael wasn't working nights, he and Maureen sometimes sat up at the kitchen table sipping black coffee and speculating about why their daughter had been chosen to undergo so much suffering. They always came up with the same answer. It was God's Will. But it was also His Will, they agreed, that had chosen them as the recipients of a priceless gift, the complete, fulfilling experience of love that they shared with their daughter. They could not have imagined the intensity of love and happiness she had brought to their lives.

Even during the worst times, the Ryan humor was also available to help them break through the suffering. Along with generous good humor, most of the Ryans were gifted with generous noses. Michael and Patty were standing together one day peering into the neonatology unit when a nurse approached them.

"Are you the mother?" she asked Patty.

Michael leaped back, shaking his head. "Oh my God," he gasped in mock alarm. "If she were the mother, we could take a graft from her nose and give Kerry a thumb."

The nurse smiled at the humor between brother and sister. "You're coping," she said.

Amazingly, as it appeared to her parents, Kerry survived the repeated operations, the tests, and the shots, and gradually began to gain strength and weight. Three months after she was admitted to Maimonides, she was carried out of the hospital in her mother's arms and driven to Michael's parents' home in Brooklyn. Doctors cautioned her parents that they should do everything possible to prevent her from crying. Her heart was not strong enough to endure the strain.

Before bringing Kerry home, Maureen was taught to monitor her heart rate, which she had to do before administering medication. She was also taught to give Kerry injections. Maureen watched intently as a doctor demonstrated how the shots were to be given. The process was uncomplicated and appeared to be simple enough, until it was time for Maureen to actually pierce her baby's sensitive skin with the needle. Kerry screamed. Maureen's stomach contracted and her throat tightened. Tears flooded her eyes, and she held tightly to her sick baby, rocking back and forth, sobbing with despair and frustration.

Both Michael and Maureen had employee insurance that provided excellent medical coverage for themselves and their families. Each policy provided for payment of eighty percent of the medical expenses of their daughter. But the costs of her hospitalization and treatment were staggering, and the twenty percent of the fees they were still liable for, as well as inevitable extras such as special nursing care, were piling up.

The first hospital bill the young couple received was for $42,000. Their share was $8,000. Michael was earning barely more than $7,900 annually at that time. And because of their middle-income salaries, they could not qualify for any form of government assistance to help pay the burgeoning medical bills. They were sliding rapidly and deeply into debt.

Michael's father, who had missed no more than a dozen days of work at the Brooklyn State Psychiatric Hospital in all the years he was employed there, agreed to take time off from his job and stay with the baby so that Maureen could return to IBM. Michael's mother had volunteered dozens of hours of special-duty nursing, providing one-on-one care for her granddaughter during periods of recovery from surgery and other crises, which eliminated additional heavy expense.

Mick Ryan didn't easily consent to becoming a full-time babysitter and nurse for Kerry. He was anxious to do anything he could for his granddaughter, but the prospect of being alone for hours with such a critically ill and fragile child, with responsibility for changing her diapers and cleaning around the colostomy, horrified him. It would have been less intimidating if Kerry was a boy. Mick Ryan was never comfortable with the idea of changing the diapers of girls.

Nevertheless he reluctantly permitted his wife to convince him that he could care for his granddaughter. She trained her husband, as she had taught Maureen, to clean the blood and feces from the colostomy. She demonstrated how he was to monitor the baby's heart beat and how to attach an infant's belly band. And she showed them both how to apply Vaseline gauze to the sensitive skin surrounding the opening, which almost constantly oozed plasma.

Nearly every night after supper Maureen and Vicky sat fashioning yards of new dressings from clean gauze and a huge jar of Vaseline. The gauze was folded and half-moons cut out of the center so that when the bandages were opened, they left perfect circles which were eventually placed over the opening of the colostomy.

The Vaseline was heated on the kitchen stove until it liquefied, then poured in stainless steel containers onto the dressings to make Vaseline gauze. Kerry's grandmother demonstrated how to pick up the bandages, one at a time with tweezers, and to place them over the colostomy so that when the feces were expelled, they collected on the material and did not irritate the sensitive skin.

Five days a week from 6:30 AM, when the front door slammed behind his wife, until 4:30 PM, when she returned, Mick Ryan was alone with the baby and with his fears. Vicky had a direct line at the hospital and didn't need to use the more time-consuming switchboard, so he could reach her easily and quickly if there was an emergency. And she telephoned him three or four times each day. But he constantly agonized over fears that something would go wrong and the baby would die while he was taking care of her. She was so tiny and delicate he worried every time he picked her up. But he walked with her in his arms and cooed Irish ballads to her for hours each day.

Although Kerry had been permitted to return home,

she was still desperately ill. She had to struggle for every breath, and her precarious health and the constant bouts of surgery had kept her from gaining more than a few ounces of weight during her first three months. It was vital that her weight be increased. But gaining weight is a difficult task for cardiac patients, especially for one so small. And even more so, for one who had atresias of the duoderm. Feet upon feet of her small intestine had to be removed, complicating her condition by decreasing her body's absorption of food.

Colostomies also inhibit food absorption, and Kerry continued to have difficulty keeping anything down. She vomited a half dozen times every day. When she refused to eat because eating made her sick, her parents and grandparents improvised and coaxed her until she permitted them to feed her tiny amounts of soft food.

It took two hours to feed Kerry two ounces of formula. Then, she usually vomited it up, shooting the food out of her mouth like a projectile. Her hunger and frustration caused her to cry, and flooded her grandfather with panic because he knew the danger that crying posed to her damaged heart. Despite his worries, however, after a few weeks Kerry appeared to be gaining strength.

Then, two months after Kerry was released from Maimonides, without warning, her weakened heart rebelled at the demands made on it and nearly failed. She was turning purple and hardly breathing when she was rushed back to the hospital. There Kerry underwent her first catheterization, a procedure designed to disclose the amount of pressure on her lungs, and the size of the tear in her heart. She later underwent the process twice more to permit doctors to determine how long they could wait before performing the open-heart surgery. It was vital to buy as much time as possible so that she could build up weight and strength.

The next time Kerry left the hospital, her grandfather took early retirement from his job so that he could care for her. Michael and Maureen left her with her grandparents in Brooklyn, but on weekends returned with her to their new house on Long Island.

During the five years that Michael and Maureen worked at IBM before Kerry's birth, they had saved $10,000. Adding a $5,000 gift from Michael's parents to their savings, they made a whopping down payment on a $29,500 two-story hi-ranch-style home in Stony Brook, Suffolk County, along Long Island's historic and picturesque North Shore.

The house was constructed with a living room, dining room, and a moderately sized kitchen and breakfast nook on the main floor. Three bedrooms, one with a fireplace, and the bath were upstairs. They moved in their furniture: bedroom sets for themselves and Kerry, and a lone green armchair. The stove and refrigerator came with the house. There was no money for additional furnishings. Kerry's health and care were their top priority.

Some time after Michael and Maureen moved, Mick and Vicky Ryan also left Brooklyn and settled into the big house in Kings Park, a few miles from Stony Brook. Kerry returned permanently to her parents' home. Michael and Maureen had missed being with their daughter evenings, and she had begun to respond to them as if they were visitors and her grandparents were her parents.

Maureen began a new job at the Kings Park Psychiatric Center as a rehabilitation trainee, and Vicky took a six-month leave of absence to take care of Kerry and work to build the baby's weight sufficiently to withstand open-heart surgery. Doctors said that eighteen pounds was the absolute minimum weight necessary before they could operate.

Vicky Ryan, meanwhile, was determined that Kerry

would have every opportunity to learn to walk. Kerry had an orthopedic cast on her arm, so she couldn't crawl before walking as most babies do. The weight of the cast made it impossible for her to balance herself, so her grandmother placed her in a playpen.

Vicky worked with her granddaughter for hours, teaching her to lower one knee and to raise the opposite foot while helping to balance herself with an arm holding on to the side of the playpen. At other times she put a Latin music record on the stereo, stuck a feather behind her ear, and danced. The baby chortled in delight and swung her arms and legs in imitation of her grandmother.

Then the baby was taught to do an exercise that her grandmother called the "showgirl kick," standing solidly on one leg while hoisting the other chest high. Vicky demonstrated the showgirl kick only while they were alone.

Vicky's mother, who was nearing eighty and experiencing difficulty with her sight, was occasionally staying at the house by that time. She played with Kerry, teaching her to clap hands and to perform other baby games such as "see the fly" and "up the nose." All this helped to keep Kerry entertained and to exercise her thin limbs, while building stamina and improving her circulation.

Kerry's grandfather was also anxious for her to walk, and when his wife returned to her job, he stepped up his efforts. Every day he would stand the baby next to a wall so that she could use it to steady herself, and patiently lead her toward him with one of his big calloused hands. When the fragile legs buckled and the baby collapsed onto her bottom, he would patiently pick her up and start her over again. Kerry was gaining both weight and self-confidence, and on her grandfather's sixtieth birthday the two of them had a surprise ready for the family.

About a dozen people, including Mick Ryan's two

brothers, were gathered on the front porch on May 25, 1972, when he called to Kerry.

"Come on now, Kerry," he coaxed, "show your mommy and daddy what you can do."

As he steadied her and nodded with his head toward her parents, she released her grip on his finger and tottered in a half dozen shaky baby steps to her mother's outstretched arms.

Kerry's doctors decided that she was strong enough to undergo the multistage operation that was necessary to avoid the possibility of contracting infections when she underwent cardiac surgery to close the hole in her heart.

Surgeons explained to her parents that they would create a rectal opening and close a fistula, an abnormal passage between the rectum and the vagina, during the initial procedures. Kerry would remain in the hospital for ten days before being allowed to return home. Two weeks later she would be readmitted so that surgeons could attach her colon to her rectum and close the colostomy.

The afternoon before Kerry was admitted to Maimonides for the new operation, Maureen spent thirty-seven dollars and fifty cents of the family's tightly budgeted funds on a Japanese maple. Kerry scampered up and down the lawn while her parents planted the tree in the front lawn. Apprehensive as always about the approaching surgery, Maureen's hopes for the life and growth of the tree were symbolic of her hopes for Kerry.

Kerry was admitted on the Labor Day weekend. Maureen snapped two photographs of her outside the hospital. Inside her parents showed her off by encouraging her to walk for the nurses. Kerry and the staff of the pediatrics ward were old friends.

Maureen was as familiar on the pediatrics ward as her

daughter. She was always with her daughter when Kerry was wheeled away for surgery, and she was always waiting when Kerry awakened from anesthesia. Maureen hugged her and held Kerry's hand when the baby was submitted to examinations and subjected to uncomfortable probings with needles. Between X-rays, EKGs, and other tests, mother and daughter played in Kerry's room or went for walks along the pediatrics ward. They came to know other children: a little girl who had lost her hair to leukemia; a little boy whose body was covered with ugly bruises and cigarette burns inflicted by his parents; and in the bed next to Kerry's, a dying baby whose parents refused to name him because their religion taught that their critically brain-damaged son was born as punishment for sins they had committed.

Maureen lingered impatiently in the waiting room until the doctors advised her that the latest operation had been completed. She telephoned Michael at home and he hurried to the hospital. Kerry was still unconscious when she was wheeled into the postoperative area. Her vital signs appeared to be stable, but she wasn't expected to regain consciousness for a few hours. Doctors said that she was apparently well, and her parents decided to drive home so that Maureen could shower, sleep for a few hours in a bed, and change into fresh clothing before returning to the hospital and resuming her vigil. They were preparing to leave when Kerry's doctor recommended that they obtain a special-duty nurse to watch over her. It was a Jewish holiday and there was none available at the Jewish Orthodox institution, so Michael telephoned his mother. They were driving from the parking lot to begin the eighty-mile trip home as she arrived. The phone was ringing when they walked into their house—it was Michael's mother, who told them to get back to the hospital as quickly as possible. Their baby was in critical condition.

When Vicky had walked into Kerry's room the doctors, the residents and a half dozen interns were huddled around the baby's bed. Her face was drawn, her body was shuddering with fine tremors, and her flaccid gray legs were jerking.

"What's the matter with her?" Kerry's grandmother demanded.

"It's an electrolyte imbalance," the doctor replied. (Body electrolytes are substances such as sodium and potassium, which are capable of carrying electrical impulses.)

The baby's grandmother had worked too long in the neurosurgery department at Brooklyn Hospital during World War II to believe that. She disagreed. "It's neurological," she said. "Just look at that child."

The doctor shook his head negatively when she advised him that she was going to be the special-duty nurse for her granddaughter. He didn't think it was a good idea. She responded by demanding to meet the special-duty nurse who was going to take her place.

"There aren't any specials," he admitted. "It's a Jewish holiday."

Kerry's grandmother slipped off her coat, pushed through the squad of residents and interns, and planted herself firmly by the side of the baby's bed. Her eyes narrowed in an indignant frown as they followed the retreating doctor and his retinue through the door.

"Electrolyte imbalance," she muttered. "Bullshit!"

Maureen was hardly aware of the ride back to the hospital. But she would never forget the fear and distress on her mother-in-law's face when she and Michael hurried into their daughter's room.

Kerry's temperature was climbing rapidly, and her

grandmother and the night nurse took turns sponging her to keep her fever down. The baby didn't talk, open her eyes, or exhibit any signs of awareness. She was in a deep coma.

A week after the surgery, Michael, Maureen, and Patty were waiting in Kerry's room for her pediatrician to arrive and explain the results of tests, when a group of interns and residents trooped inside and examined her. Patty followed them out of the room and asked a resident what had happened to Kerry. He said he believed she had neurological damage.

Maureen's mother joined the family in the room, and they waited throughout the remainder of the day and into the night before Kerry's pediatrician arrived at 11 PM. Summoning them into another room, he confirmed the resident's diagnosis. He explained that during surgery Kerry had suffered an embolism that traveled through the hole in her heart to her brain. If it had not been for the hole, the blood clot would have entered her lungs and killed her.

The pediatrician was unable to assure the family that Kerry would live. And he couldn't predict what degree of recovery she would achieve if she did survive. Maureen fled from the room.

Mick Ryan was waiting in the parking lot when his wife walked up to the car he was in. Tears were streaming down her cheeks as she told him about Kerry. His body jerked as if he had been slapped, and he lifted his forearm over his eyes. It couldn't protect him from the anguish.

"For the love of Jesus, don't tell me anymore," he moaned. "You're devastating me. I had her walking and I thought she would at least get something out of life just being able to go to the bathroom by herself. Now what's ahead for the poor little baby!"

As soon as Maureen got home, she trudged upstairs and

flopped exhaustedly onto her bed. There was no escape in sleep. She dreamed about burying Kerry's damaged body. She awakened with a start and a cry. Sweat poured from her. As Michael held her close and comforted her, she recognized the symbolism of the dream. Michael's refusal to help bury the child fit in with his refusal to give up. And Kerry's struggle to keep her head exposed corresponded with her continuing fight for love and survival.

Kerry continued in a deep coma. Her parents, grandmothers and other family members once more spent hours in silent vigil seated or standing by her bed. Occasionally they reached over the limp body and gently stroked the smooth skin or studied her eyes for a sign of movement and recognition. Kerry's expression never changed, and her eyes never moved.

Michael left the room one day to walk along the hall and stretch his muscles while Maureen remained seated beside Kerry's bed. Her eyes were shadowed by fatigue and worry as she peered forlornly at her daughter and wondered if the baby's suffering would ever end. Perhaps it would be impossible to love so deeply without experiencing such intense pain, she speculated. Impulsively she leaned over the bed and kissed the silent infant, an act she had performed a hundred times before. Without consciously planning to, she began caressing her baby and softly reciting a children's poem:

> We're going on a treasure hunt.
> X marks the spot.
> Up and down, and around and around,
> With a pinch and a squeeze,
> And an ocean breeze.

As Maureen crooned the lines, she gently traced her finger across Kerry's chest. When she recited "X marks the spot," she tapped her finger on Kerry's chest. The "ocean breeze" was accentuated by her softly blowing on Kerry's cheek and face.

Maureen felt the response before she saw it. Drawing on that mysterious psychic bond between mother and child, she suddenly knew that Kerry understood. Then, as she watched, Kerry's lips began ever so slowly to form into a hesitant smile.

Maureen burst out of her chair and ran into the hallway, yelling for her husband. Startled, then curious, nurses stopped and peered at her. Michael was using a wall telephone, and he left the receiver dangling. There had been so many emergencies, so many crises, when both were certain their baby was going to die. Fear flooded his system with adrenalin as he rushed to the room. Abruptly he realized that this time there was nothing to fear. The tears in his wife's eyes were formed by happiness.

Maureen was afraid that Kerry wouldn't smile again. She leaned over the bed and began softly whispering the poem once more. Kerry smiled!

The drive to Stony Brook that night was a celebration. They held hands, described Kerry's smile to each other, and repeatedly assured one another that after all their troubles, everything was finally going to be all right.

It was days before they admitted their fears about Kerry's eyes. As they sat by her bedside telling her stories, murmuring the poem, and watching for her smile, they were finally forced to concede that although she had regained consciousness, her eyes never followed them. Her eyes did not appear to have any sensitivity to light.

There were more tests. Doctors advised Michael and Maureen that the blood clot had destroyed her vision. She was totally blind. To her mother, blindness was the most distressing of all Kerry's handicaps. How could Kerry participate in a world she couldn't see?

Kerry's condition slipped from guarded to critical, to stable and back to critical with roller coaster speed. Maureen spent days and nights in the bland and dreary hospital room, until exhaustion finally overtook her and she curled up in a chair for a few hours sleep. She was always careful to awaken before 6 AM so that she would have time to wash and dress before the day-shift nurses and doctors came on duty. But one morning she overslept, and when she awoke the room was full of doctors and interns. Startled, she tried to stand up before untangling her legs from the chair, and toppled over in an embarrassed heap at their feet.

Doctors were worried about the limpness of Kerry's body. During examinations, when they lifted one of her arms and released it, the arm flopped listlessly back down beside her. Her body was unnaturally limp, and she couldn't sit up or support her own head without help. She was eighteen months old and functioning on the level of an eight-week-old infant. Doctors eventually concluded that the embolism had severely damaged the motor area of her brain. It would be difficult for her to control her arms and legs, and she might not ever be able to talk.

Three and one half months after the embolism, Kerry was taken home. She was curled in a fetal position, barely able to breathe without assistance, and the doctors were pessimistic about her chances of survival. She was still desperately ill, but if she was going to die, her parents decided that it would be at home, surrounded by family who loved her.

Along with her daughter, Maureen carried home two pages of instructions, ten medical prescriptions, and orders to give the little girl injections every six hours.

Kerry cried constantly, and it worried her parents. The hole in her heart still hadn't been repaired, and her slender hold on life was so tenuous that a crying spell considered normal for another baby could kill Kerry.

As for most babies, Kerry's bottle was an almost surefire remedy for crying. A bottle and a back rub could usually be counted on to quiet her for a few hours.

She was kept on a bottle longer than most babies because her weakened heart made it dangerous to spoonfeed her. Eating solids would have been too much of an exertion for her, so her food was put into a blender until it was sufficiently broken down to be poured into a bottle. A large hole was cut in the rubber nipple so that she could suck her food out.

Her parents were alarmed when her doctor informed them that it was time to end the bottle feedings. Visions of her screaming and crying for her bottle until she suffered cardiac arrest haunted Maureen during the eighty-mile trip home to Stony Brook from Brooklyn. But the concern was unjustified; there was no crisis.

Michael and Maureen learned they could make her more comfortable and quiet her if they held her in their arms and rubbed her back while walking with her. Unable to see or to do anything for herself, she desperately needed the reassurance of close and loving contact with another human. They walked with her for hours, trading off with each other when they were tired. Their friend, Joe Duquette, also often walked with her.

A husky, tightly built man of enormous energy, Duquette had quickly become Michael's closest friend on the Suffolk County Police Department. A bachelor who professed to be uncomfortable around children, he was actu-

ally refreshingly sensitive and caring. And he was loyal to
his friends.

Duquette was aware of the difficulties his friends were
undergoing with their sick daughter, and Kerry soon
learned to recognize the secure feeling of snuggling in the
arms of the big man as he patiently paced the kitchen
floor with her, gently rubbing her tiny back, or hoisting
her across his broad chest and shoulders and softly tapping the blankets across her bottom until she stopped
crying.

The Ryans still had only the single green armchair in
the house, and during Duquette's frequent visits there
was always a race for the prize. The losers stretched out
uncomfortably on the hard living room floor. It was like
lying on concrete.

When he was home, Michael repeatedly stroked
Kerry's face and whispered to her about the good times
they shared before she became so ill and how she had
learned to call him "Da-da." He was determined that she
would begin talking, despite the doctors' doubts. Michael
petted and cooed to her for hours, but the bright blue eyes
never wavered. They always stared straight ahead, unsee-
ing and unblinking. Maureen was watching one night as
he was again urging Kerry to talk. "Come on," he coaxed,
"say Da-da. I know you can do it, because I love you."

"Da-da."

The word was whispered ever so lightly. Then the tiny
mouth formed into a smile and the word was formed
again. "Da-da." This time it was louder.

Michael was on his feet hugging her to his chest, danc-
ing in a circle and excitedly telling Kerry how much he
and her mother loved her, and how proud they were.
Maureen ran to the telephone and began calling her

mother and Michael's parents. Struggling to speak through happy tears, she sobbed out the good news. Kerry was talking.

Michael and Maureen began to permit themselves to hope that when the pressure on Kerry's brain was relieved, she might regain her sight. But although she continued to talk and added exciting new words to her vocabulary, her eyes remained blank.

Victoria Ryan purchased bright balloons and painted faces on them to give to her granddaughter, hoping they would help accomplish a breakthrough. Mick Ryan sat for hours, moving a small flashlight back and forth in front of Kerry's eyes, always hoping to entice her pupils to dilate or to follow the beam. At other times, he fashioned rag dolls for her and tempted her with red and green feathers, always taking care to select the brightest colors he could find.

Maureen began experiencing medical problems of her own. She had been troubled with bronchial asthma since childhood, and it was getting worse. She was taken to the emergency rooms of hospitals a couple of times when the attacks became especially severe. Yet another time, she was hospitalized to have a benign tumor removed from her breast.

Yet concern for Kerry's health and welfare continued to dominate the family's thinking and lives. Just as they had determined that Kerry would talk, Michael and Maureen were determined that she would see again. Besides the hours shining a flashlight at her eyes to stimulate them, Michael and Duquette often struck matches or flicked a lighter and moved the flame past Kerry's eyes, while watching hopefully for movement or dilation of the pupils.

One night, as Michael was watching Kerry's eyes and shining the flashlight at her, he thought he detected a

slight change in the size of the pupils. Maureen agreed.
The pupils were dilating. Kerry could detect light.

When they told her doctors about their discovery, the
physicians were firm. It was time for Kerry's family to face
the truth, they declared. She would never see again.
Kerry's cardiologist was so frustrated he yelled at them,
warning that their continued refusal to accept their
daughter's blindness would only impede efforts to help
her with therapy.

Michael and Maureen nevertheless refused to give up.
With their friend Duquette, and Mick and Vicky, they
continued working with the lights and the matches—up
to the time Kerry was hospitalized again in 1973—this
time to close the colostomy and to attach her bowels to
her rectum.

As usual, the Ryans were broke. Their share of Kerry's
medical expenses after insurance, and the auxiliary costs
were staggering. Dental care alone accounted for major
expenses. Dentists were afraid to work on Kerry's teeth
because of the delicate condition of her heart, so every
time a cavity had to be filled, she was taken to a hospital
and placed under general anesthesia. Her first dental bill,
for care of baby teeth, was $700. Her baby teeth were in
poor condition, but her parents had them silver capped to
protect the spaces for her permanent teeth.

Maureen had again settled in at Kerry's hospital bedside, and she was hungry. Kerry would be fed in about an
hour, and Maureen was looking forward to slipping a few
bites of food off her daughter's tray. Kerry never finished
her food.

Maureen reached for her empty wallet hoping to find
some forgotten change. As she rummaged inside, her
hand closed on a tightly rolled wad of currency. It
amounted to two hundred dollars and had obviously been
left there by Duquette.

Kerry was sleeping one day when Maureen slipped out of the room and walked down the hall to the hospital cafeteria. She was returning to the room in the pediatric ward when Kerry's cardiologist rushed up and threw his arms around her. Then he stepped back, grinned, and announced, "I've come to eat crow."

"What in the world are you talking about?" she asked, startled.

"I was just in to see Kerry," he declared. "And she can see!"

"Yeah, I know," Maureen retorted, unable to completely erase the smugness from her voice. "We've been telling you that."

Kerry had been blind for eighteen months, almost exactly half her life. Medical experts agreed that patients like her did not regain their sight. But she had.

Kerry was also holding her head up by herself and showing encouraging signs of being able to exert some control over her limbs when she was returned to the hospital to have the colostomy closed. It was to be her first bout with surgery since the embolism. Her parents were cautioned there was a chance of another embolism occurring while anesthesia was being administered for the new operation.

The waiting was excruciating. This time, however, there was no trouble with embolisms. Trouble occurred, instead, when the IV began to flow freely into the tissues and to infiltrate the body's cells. IVs are the lifelines of surgical patients, and when they slip out of the vein, it is imperative that they be reattached quickly.

Members of the surgical team worked frantically and unsuccessfully to reattach the IV to the vein in Kerry's arm. In desperation they cut directly into the jugular vein.

After surgery they began a relatively new but increasingly used process called hyperalimentation, introducing high-protein carbohydrates, fats, and trace elements—a solution far superior to traditional IV feedings—directly into the little girl's bloodstream via the jugular. Eventually she would undergo the operation, called a cut-down by hospital personnel, more than twenty times. Each time, her mother was beside her, squeezing her hand while surgeons made the incision, separated the skin with mosquito clamps, and reached inside with tweezers to lift up the tiny vein so that the needle could be inserted before the wound was sutured.

Kerry survived the operation and began to rapidly regain strength. After she had undergone ten days of postoperative care without complications, her parents began to admit feelings of cautious optimism and to talk of taking her home in a few days.

On the eleventh day after the operation, Kerry's temperature shot up to a death-threatening 107 degrees. Anticonvulsion drugs were administered, she was covered with specially cooled sheets and blankets, and other efforts were made to reduce her temperature. Nothing worked. When she was placed in an oxygen tent, her parents, grandparents, and aunts reached inside to stroke her, cuddle her, and whisper encouragement.

Doctors diagnosed the trouble as a candida infection. The infection usually means death for seriously ill adults who contract it, and it is even more virulent to children. Candida is caused by bacteria that everyone carries, and is generally harmless to anyone except hosts who are in severely weakened condition. Someone such as Kerry Ryan.

The site of the infection appeared to be the incision made in Kerry's jugular to feed her. She hovered on the edge of life for fifteen days. Maureen stayed at the hospital round-the-clock, sleeping there and eating all of her meals inside.

She had already planned how she would tell Michael if Kerry died. She had decided she would take a taxi to the nearest police precinct and ask one of the officers to drive her to Stony Brook so that she could personally break the news to her husband. Doctors repeatedly reaffirmed the graveness of Kerry's condition, and she was constantly in danger of congestive heart failure.

The Ryans handled their problems by planning ahead, and by supporting each other. Maureen knew that if they lost Kerry, she and Michael would cope with the grief together. She went over her plans. It was like teaching children with fire drills. One hoped the fire evacuation plan never had to be used in a real emergency, but there had to be a plan just in case.

Maureen never had to ask for the ride to Stony Brook. Kerry fought off the infection, and two months after surgery she returned home again. And once again, the Ryan and O'Connor families closed in to support each other while Kerry gained strength for the next operation.

When there was trouble, there was always Duquette, a member of Michael's family, or someone from Maureen's family anxious to help. There were also times when help came from other policemen who worked with Michael— or from strangers.

When doctors said that Kerry needed more exercise to strengthen her heart, the Ryans built a 40' x 20' pool in their back yard with money they were hoarding to replace their old Volkswagen, which had logged nearly 100,000 miles and was failing fast. Don Pawson, a policeman friend who moonlighted selling and installing pools, sold Michael the pool at cost and then installed it. There was still only one straight-backed chair in the Ryan house. The pool was a necessity, not a luxury.

A few years later when Kerry was hospitalized for open-heart surgery, officers from another precinct pooled all the money they planned to spend for Christmas cards and postage, made out a check, and presented it to Michael and Maureen to help with medical expenses. They had never worked with Michael.

The Ryans deducted so much mileage for medical expenses from their income tax—never less than 50,000 miles annually for two years—they were audited four times, twice in one year, by the Internal Revenue Service.

One Christmas Eve the Ryans answered a knock at their front door and were confronted by a man and his wife who were strangers to them. The couple had a re-built wheelchair for Kerry. They explained it was a gift from the maintenance staff at the IRS office. The chair was equipped with a horn, a doll tied to one side, and ten dollars—left over from the collection—was in an envelope attached to the other side.

Late in 1973 doctors decided that it was time for the operation on her heart. Kerry was gaining strength and self confidence, but her damaged heart was an ever-present threat to her existence. Because of her weakened physical condition, she was susceptible to all manner of colds and other diseases. She had pneumonia several times, and once contracted scarlet fever—a relatively rare disease today.

Kerry had seen more than enough of hospitals, but her mother explained that the new operation could not be avoided. She promised the little girl that the interminable chain of operations was almost completed.

Kerry was admitted to New York University Hospital in Manhattan. The preoperative medicine Kerry was given in her room did not make her lose consciousness, and when an orderly came for her with a stretcher, she clung to her mother crying, "Tell them no." Maureen gently disengaged Kerry's arms and placed her on the stretcher. She watched helplessly as Kerry was wheeled, crying, toward the elevator.

Maureen phoned Michael at home to tell him Kerry had been taken to surgery. As the surgical team toiled over the child, repairing the hole in her heart and covering it with a dacron patch, Maureen drank coffee and flipped aimlessly through magazines on the pediatrics ward. Michael nervously chewed and puffed on a slim cigar during the long lonely hours at Stony Brook. It was the first time he had used tobacco since before Kerry's birth, and it marked the resumption of his smoking habit.

Accompanied by a nurse, Maureen walked unsurely through the door of the intensive-care recovery room hours later and stared with tired eyes at the chalk-white face of the child lying on the oversize stretcher. Kerry's mouth was distended grotesquely by the respirator forced inside it, an EKG monitor was continuously beeping, and lifelines extended from her body in every direction like plastic spiderwebs. A doctor and a nurse assigned especially to Kerry were taking medical readings. Maureen was shocked at the length of the near chest-to-navel incision. Her eyes swept over the ugly scars on the little body. Insidiously a question intruded into her consciousness: "Did I do anything while I was pregnant to cause all of this pain?" It was a question that had plagued her before, and she shook it from her mind.

Silently, her eyes stinging, she leaned over and gently

kissed Kerry on the cheek. The quiet little figure was unnaturally cold, her skin like transparent china. There was no response to the mother's kiss. The nurse said it was time to go, and Maureen rushed from the room.

Ten days later Kerry was back home, apparently recovering from her latest ordeal without complications. But in three more weeks her breathing suddenly became erratic again, the pink left her cheeks, and the ominous blue shadows returned around her lips and eyes. The dacron patch had developed a leak. Doctors explained that tissue might yet grow over the newest opening. The family waited, and eventually Kerry's appetite and weight increased. The healthy color returned.

The little girl never stopped fighting. "She's tough as nails, a gritty, tough kid," her father once remarked to his friend Duquette after Kerry had once again survived a medical crisis expected to take her life. "If she had to get out of the house and the only way out was through concrete, she'd chew her way through."

Kerry was still only three years old when she was enrolled at a rehabilitation center. It proved a trying time for her. The quality of the care that Kerry received there was not acceptable to her family. Afternoons when she returned home from classes, she was soaked to her waist. Her grandfather would meet the bus at 3 PM, and as he lifted Kerry into his arms, urine would dribble down his shirt and trousers. Maureen began marking her daughter's diapers so that she could tell if they were changed during the day. Mick Ryan advised the bus driver that the diapers were being marked and if they weren't changed, he would soon be making a call on the school faculty.

More than a year later Kerry's parents, grandparents,

and aunts finally visited the school en masse to confront the principal and staff. The Ryans learned that Kerry was the only child in the classroom who was both immobile and incontinent. She was apparently being changed behind a screen once a day before lunch. Her classmates could either see her, or were at least aware that she had to wear a diaper and be cared for like an infant. After lunch, she was apparently permitted to sit in any urine or feces she produced.

Physical therapy was provided for Kerry twice a week in the hallway where nonhandicapped children regularly passed and made fun of her. Her family insisted that she needed her diapers changed more often and in private surroundings. And she needed therapy daily in an area where she would not be exposed to the cruel taunts of other children. They were accused of blaming the staff because Kerry was not functioning as normally as a nonhandicapped child her age.

Kerry's care at the school improved, nevertheless. She was one of the lucky ones, a physically challenged child— she and her parents avoided the word handicapped— with an extended family that had become her support system. From the beginning Kerry's fight for life, and her rehabilitation, had been a total family effort.

On two occasions she was taken to holy shrines of the Catholic church by her family, first to Lourdes by her mother, then to the shrine of St. Anne de Beaupré near Quebec.

Mick Ryan had climbed the stairs of St. Anne on his knees, carrying his granddaughter in his arms. When he turned to her and told her that they were going to climb all the way to the top, she asked him if she would walk again when they reached the summit. He sadly admitted that he didn't know.

The old man and the little girl were met at the top of

the stairs by an old priest who promised to pray for Kerry. But she didn't walk.

The trips occurred during a low point in their emotions and morale. Kerry's operations were coming with such unceasing regularity, creating one crisis after another, that Michael and Maureen were emotionally and physically exhausted. They had been raised with a strong and abiding faith in their religion, but for a time the tragedy of Kerry's crippling birth defects had shaken the faith of almost everyone in the family, except Mick.

Still, Kerry's health appeared to have improved somewhat, but she continued to be plagued by bladder infections. Doctors at first explained that she had a reflux, which meant that when urine was released from the bladder, it caused a spasm that sent the fluid back into the kidneys, causing infection. But X-rays taken during the round of medical examinations disclosed that the problem was much more serious. Kerry had a neurogenic bladder. If the earlier diagnosis had been accurate, the condition could have been corrected with surgery. But a neurogenic bladder could not be.

The new diagnosis was crushing and infuriating. It meant that Kerry's condition had been misdiagnosed when she was an infant. For years her parents had told her that her incontinence could be corrected with a relatively simple operation. Now they were being told her condition was inoperable and that she would be in diapers as long as she lived.

The family wanted a second medical opinion and decided to contact Dr. Robert Schultz, a pediatric cardiologist in Florida who had taken his residency at Johns Hopkins University Hospital in Baltimore, and was related by marriage to the Ryan family. Kerry's parents had learned long ago that you tend to receive more attention and efficient care in hospitals if you are recommended by someone. Dr. Schultz referred them to the chief of the neurological department at Johns Hopkins, and a few days later Maureen flew to Baltimore with her daughter.

As she always did, Maureen remained with Kerry during the examination, reassuringly squeezing her daughter's hand and frequently leaning over to murmur a comforting word. Then she accompanied her to the operating room for tests on her bladder.

Only a half dozen members of the medical team, Kerry, and Maureen—who was standing next to her daughter at the head of the operating table—were in the room when a colored dye was introduced into the little girl's body with a catheter. The internal organs in Kerry's pelvic region were reflected on a huge screen nearby.

It was immediately obvious to the doctors that the diagnosis made in New York was correct. Kerry had a neurogenic bladder. It was no more able to function properly than if she had been paralyzed.

Because of Kerry's undeveloped sacrum, her bladder did not receive the necessary messages from nerves when it was time for it to be emptied. The same congenital defect also prevented Kerry from knowing when it was time to empty her bowels. Control of her feces was further complicated by a lack of sphincter muscles, which regulate closing of openings to the intestinal tract.

Maureen was still attempting to comprehend the information about Kerry's bladder when she realized that one of the doctors was counting: "Two vaginas . . . two cervixes . . . two uteruses . . . four ovaries . . ." Kerry's internal organs were still reflected on the screen, and the medical team was checking her reproductive system. She had double organs.

Maureen closed her eyes and squeezed Kerry's shoul-

der. Her mind was racing, confused, desperately wanting
to disbelieve. There had already been so much pain for
Kerry. "This can't be happening to us," Maureen silently
assured herself. But it was.

There would have to be more operations. The extra
organs would have to be removed surgically. One of the
uteri was pressing against the ureter. The pressure would
become greater and the problems increased by the time
Kerry entered an early puberty—when she was seven.

Options to a lifetime in diapers for Kerry were discussed between Maureen and members of the medical
team. A pacemakerlike device could be implanted just
under the surface of the skin and could be used to stimulate the bladder to empty itself two or three times daily.
But the pacemakers are often painful for children, and
Kerry's bladder was too small to offer much immediate
chance of a successful operation. None of the other options offered much hope of significant improvement in
her condition. She would have to wait and hope that
within a few years new satisfactory procedures might be
developed to deal with neurogenic bladders, Maureen
was told.

Orthopedic surgeons at Johns Hopkins also examined
Kerry's right hand and arm. The appearance of the arm
and hand could be radically improved with surgery, they
recommended. Enhancing the appearance of her arm
and hand could be an important step in improving her self
confidence and self image. Surgery was scheduled for a
few weeks later.

A few days before Maureen was to return to Johns Hopkins with her daughter for the operation, Kerry developed an upper respiratory infection. Michael and Maureen questioned whether or not the infection would

prevent her from undergoing the surgery on her arm and hand. Money was too scarce to risk spending it on round-trip air fare to Baltimore if the operation had to be postponed while Kerry was sent home to recover from a cold.

They decided to have her examined by a local doctor to determine if the cold would interfere with the surgery. The offices of her regular pediatrician were in Brooklyn so Maureen telephoned the Suffolk County Medical Society and asked them to recommend someone in the neighborhood. She was given the name of a general practitioner.

It was a rainy, blustery day, and as Maureen drove to the doctor's office she was thankful that she had been able to avoid the tiring round trip to Brooklyn.

As the doctor examined Kerry, Maureen told him about the scheduled operation. After he completed the examination, Maureen helped her daughter put her blouse back on and then stepped into another room for a conference.

The physician stared at Maureen for what seemed to be a long time. He was obviously choosing his words carefully.

"I'm going to be very blunt with you, Mrs. Ryan," he finally began.

Maureen had heard bad news from doctors before, and assumed she could handle it. But when the doctor spoke again, his words caught her unprepared.

"If she were mine," he said of Kerry, "I'd take her out in the rain and let her catch a bad cold. And I'd let it get worse. Why throw good money after bad?"

Maureen was stunned. She couldn't believe what she was hearing. She thought of the incredible amount of love Kerry had brought to so many people and of how she had become more precious and dear to the family than they could ever have imagined.

Kerry had struggled so tenaciously for life and everyone

around her had tried so hard to help her; it was unbeliev-able that a man trained to save lives could be so crude and cruel. Maureen's shock was replaced by anger. She was furious, and her face flushed with the intensity of her emotion.

"Who are you," she demanded of the smug physician, "to judge the quality of life?"

There was no reply. She hardly remembered snatching up Kerry, bundling her in a coat, and rushing from the office. But she remembered being outside. That was when the tension in her cheeks and the angry fire in her eyes were replaced by hurt.

Maureen postponed the trip to Baltimore for a week while she treated Kerry's cold. Mother and daughter then flew again to Baltimore and Kerry was admitted to Johns Hopkins for orthopedic surgery on her hand and arm.

During that operation and a subsequent procedure, the twisted right hand was realigned in closer conformity with her shortened arm. A long metal pin was inserted at the wrist until the flesh and bone damaged during surgery healed.

Kerry was hospitalized nearly a month. The Ryans were broke again, and as she had done many times before, Maureen spent most of her nights curled up on a chair in a dreary hospital room next to her little girl's bed. Once a week Maureen rented a motel room, took a shower, and slept in a bed.

About a week after Kerry returned home, she had a bad day, crying and fussing. It was something she had almost never done since the end of her trouble retaining food. It was almost dinnertime when Maureen realized that Kerry's cast was slipping down her hand, covering her fingers. Maureen took the cast off.

That was when she learned what was causing Kerry's discomfort. The metal pin had moved and was coming through the skin. Kerry was taken to Mather Hospital in Port Jefferson, L.I., where the pin was removed. Her orthopedic surgeon at Johns Hopkins used a telephone hookup to advise the surgeon in the operating room and lead him step by step through the surgical process.

Kerry was delighted with her new arm. But she had had enough of operations.

"No more needles," she told her parents, shaking her head. "No more."

Michael Ryan in Vietnam, August 1967.

A C-123 spraying defoliants in South Vietnam, in an official U.S. Air Force photograph (1966).

(Above, left) Chris Johnson, founder of Vietnam Veterans of South Dakota. (courtesy of Rapid City *Journal*)

(Below, left) Vietnam veteran Paul Reutershan on his civilian job as a train conductor.

(Above, right) Paul Reutershan's grave. (Jeff Blechman)

(Below, right) Frank McCarthy, of Agent Orange Victims International. (Jeff Blechman)

PAUL M. REUTERSHAN
MAR. 24, 1950 ✝ DEC. 14, 1978

UNSELFISHLY YOU GAVE IN YOUR TIME
OF SUFFERING SO THAT OTHERS MIGHT
BE SAVED. THIS GIFT SHALL STAND AS
A TESTAMENT OF YOUR COURAGE,
STRENGTH AND FAITH.
FRIEND OF THE EARTH; LOVER OF LIFE.
YOU KNOW THE JOY OF BEING ONE
WITH GOD.

Joan Maiman, Chairman of the Veterans' Leadership Conference. (Cliff Linedecker)

Maude DeVictor wearing an Agent Orange sweatshirt. (Jeff Blechman)

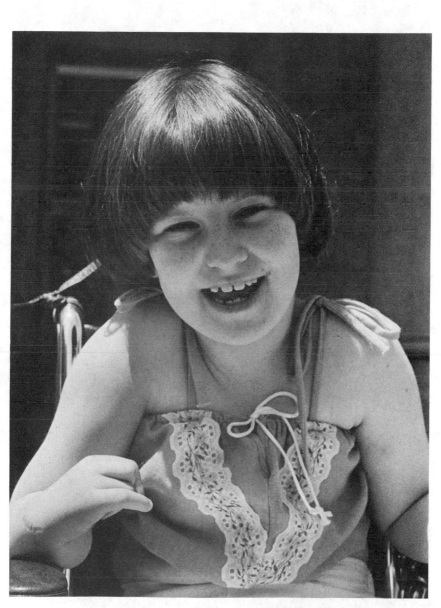

Kerry Ryan, at eight years of age. (Jeff Blechman)

Michael and Maureen Ryan testifying about the effects of Agent Orange before a Congressional subcommittee in 1979. (Jeff Blechman)

Michael Ryan conferring with environmental lawyer Victor Yannacone. (Jeff Blechman)

Maureen Ryan and Kerry at a Congressional hearing. (Jeff Blechman)

Kerry Ryan and paralyzed Vietnam veteran Bobby Muller, Chairman of the Council of Vietnam Veterans, after a Congressional hearing in 1979. (Jeff Blechman)

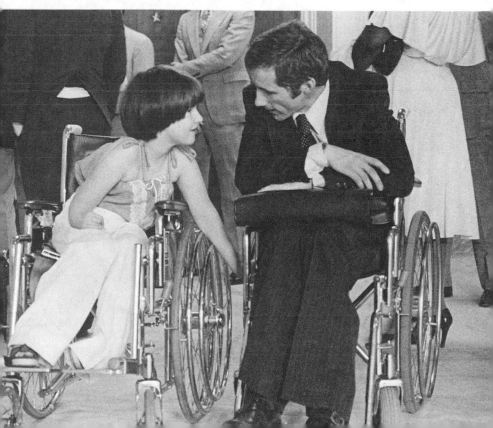

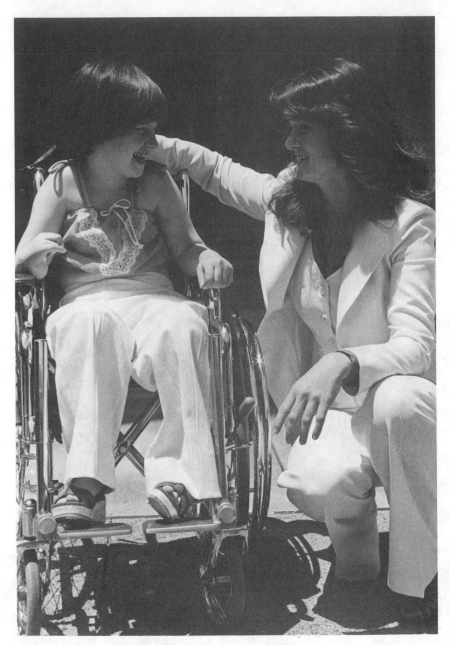

Kerry and her mother. (Jeff Blechman)

6

AGENT ORANGE

Paul Reutershan picked up the
rock and showed us the worms and
ugly creatures underneath. Then
he died . . .

Michael F. Ryan

For the first time since Kerry's birth, life began to return
to normal for the Ryans. Kerry's damaged heart was repaired, her arm and hand were reconstructed, and
the continuous bouts of surgery appeared to have
finally ended for a time. It would be years before it was
time to perform surgery on her duplicate reproductive
organs.

Kerry was six years old. She was enrolled in a local
school, where she could get regular exposure to other
children. Despite her adjustment to her conditions, she
continued to experience problems. Her eyesight was less
than perfect. She had a perceptual problem as well as no
peripheral vision. And she had to be carried upstairs at
night and downstairs in the morning. Initially that was
merely an inconvenience, but as Kerry grew and gained
weight, it developed into a more serious problem. The
house had been designed for a family with a child who

could walk, and they knew that someday they would have
to move.

Maureen's brother Brian was still spending his summers
and holidays with his sister and brother-in-law, and he was
growing up. He was in his early teens and had been staying with them for only a couple of days at the beginning
of his summer vacation when a truck stopped outside the
house and the driver delivered a new air conditioner.
Brian had worked all winter to earn the money. The next
summer, when Maureen's washing machine broke, Brian
surprised her with a new one. Yet he also managed to save
money from his jobs to help put himself through John Jay
College in Manhattan a few years later, where he majored
in criminal justice.

Michael's baby sister, Deirdre, was attending college,
working on twin master's degrees in remedial reading
and special education. She was taking classes at a reading
clinic on Long Island, and at times slept over and babysat
at her brother's house. It was she who assumed responsibility for developing her niece's social graces. Deirdre
helped turn Kerry into a gourmet when other children
her age were asking for Big Macs.

Deirdre was still living at home before Kerry's fateful
colostomy surgery, and had often taken her out for strolls.
When the baby had first come home unable to see, walk,
or talk, her Aunt Dee vowed that if Kerry ever improved
and regained her sight, she would be taught how to be-
have in restaurants, at the theater, at museums, and on
the beach. Deirdre was intent on helping improve the
quality of her niece's life. It was important, she reasoned,
to build up Kerry's self image and to teach her to interact
with other children and adults as an equal.

Beginning with their first trip together to a restaurant,

Kerry was taught to take responsibility for her own food selections. At first Kerry merely pointed at the menu. Deirdre always assured her that she had made an excellent choice, and told the waiter they had decided on whatever food Kerry pointed to.

Gradually Kerry began to differentiate between such entrees as seafood, steaks, and chops and to learn about appetizers and desserts. As her speech became more sophisticated, she began asking for the food by name. Deirdre carried a small knife and a short fork in a cellophane bag inside her purse, and Kerry used them instead of the larger, more awkward implements already set in place at the table.

Initially, whenever she was confronted by a stranger, such as a waiter or waitress, Kerry curled up, hunched over, and stuck her fingers in her mouth. Gradually she began to learn that the strangers were there to help her. She began ordering her food with more confidence and looked forward to the encounters.

Kerry also learned about tipping. Friendly, courteous service earned a larger tip than lack of attention or rudeness. And she learned to cope with people who stared at her when her aunt carried her inside a restaurant or a museum which was not constructed to accommodate wheelchairs.

When children asked questions about Kerry's arm, thumb, or about her wheelchair, Deirdre was patient with explanations. She realized that it was natural childish curiosity that prompted their questions. She was always careful to include Kerry in the conversation and made sure that her niece participated as fully as she could, depending on the verbal skills she possessed at the time.

Deirdre was less patient with adults. A maitre d' once approached her in a crowded restaurant and criticized her for spoiling Kerry by carrying her instead of allowing her to walk. Deirdre continued into the restaurant, seated her niece, and explained to her that the maitre d' was confused and didn't understand that Kerry couldn't walk. Then she excused herself, explaining that she was going to ask about the specials on the menu. Deirdre approached the maitre d' and pointed out to him that Kerry could not walk. She suggested further that he be more considerate of other handicapped children or adults who visited the restaurant.

Kerry's grandfather also took her for long strolls in her wheelchair, along the boardwalk on Long Island Sound. It was quiet and private, but almost every day they met an old priest named Father McCormick, who had suffered a heart attack and took daily walks for exercise. Father McCormick and Kerry became good friends, and she looked forward to their meetings. Invariably he would lean over and ask if she had a kiss for him. She always did. He also sometimes turned to her grandfather, creased his face into a puzzled frown, pointed and asked, "Who's that guy?"

Kerry always pretended shock. "Don't you know Mick?" she asked in return, allowing herself to giggle as her face crinkled with the pleasure of the game.

Father McCormick one day told Mick and Kerry that he was going to Rome, and he promised to ask the Holy Father to pray for her. He died there of a heart attack.

The pleasant strolls along the boardwalk with his grandchild were pleasurable for Mick Ryan. But there were times when Kerry did things or said things that choked him with emotion and helplessness.

One of those times occurred as they were passing a stately Catholic church and she asked him to stop.

"Mick, let's go in," she suggested. "Maybe He's there

and He'll make me walk." Inside she peered along the pews and stared hopefully at the altar and sacristy. Then she shook her head and disappointedly murmured, "He's not here."

At the Kings Park Psychiatric Center, Maureen became involved first in patient therapy as an aide and later in nonmedical care for the ward residents (Patty was also working at Kings Park as a supervisor of nurses). Maureen and Michael were attending night classes at the Suffolk County Community College. She had resumed her marketing courses, and he was collecting credits in both pre-law and in other courses designed to sharpen his police skills. Some of Michael's tuition was paid by the GI Bill.

For the first time in years, they could make some long-range plans for the future. Michael took the examination for sergeant, and they began planning for Maureen to graduate with a degree in marketing so that she could obtain a higher paying job and help him complete law school. There was even cautious consideration of having another baby, a brother or sister for Kerry. The idea of another baby in the house was an appealing one.

In the meantime Michael concentrated on his police work. If there was a letdown after the years of almost daily crises in his homelife, it was offset by his work. The job of a policeman was never boring. Calls varied from the ridiculous to the tragic, to the routine—and dangerous.

Michael once took the car keys from a belligerent drunk who was so intoxicated he crawled out of a tavern on his hands and knees, heading toward his parked car. The drunk punched a police sergeant and kicked a lieutenant before he was wrestled into his cell. Then he shocked the assembled policemen by unfastening an artificial leg and chucking it at Michael like a spear.

On another occasion Michael drove on a fire call at about 6:30 one morning and found a house in flames with a woman running through the front yard screaming, "My babies, my babies." By chance he had walked through the same house a few days before and observed two boys, two and three years old, while he was investigating a complaint of a vicious dog in the neighborhood. But when he responded to the fire call there, the children were nowhere in sight.

Michael sprinted into the house and was immediately confronted by a wall of smoke and heat. He crouched, then eased himself completely to the floor, and began crawling toward the bedrooms of the ranch-style home. As he pushed open the door to the first bedroom, flames leaped at him, burning the hair off the side of his head and singeing his uniform. He thought of the bullets in his police revolver and of those stored in his belt, worried that they might become hot enough to explode. He had to retreat.

By the time he had crawled to safety, he was vomiting. But he staggered to the garden hose, drenched himself, and lurched back inside the burning building. He pulled the garden hose after him. An explosion ripped through the far end of the house, and a moment later Michael lapsed into semiconsciousness, overcome by smoke and poisonous gases released from burning foam-rubber mattresses. Volunteer firemen arrived and dragged him to safety.

Michael was receiving oxygen when he revived and began yelling for the children.

"Take it easy," a policeman reassured him. "The kids are safe. They were next door all the time."

"But she was yelling to save her babies," Michael protested.

"Yeah, I know. That was her puppies. And they got out

okay. In fact," the other policeman said, pointing, "there's one of them now."

Michael turned his head. A brown puppy was just lifting its leg to water the tire on his squad car.

Michael was taken to a hospital for emergency outpatient treatment. The next day he returned when he became sick again. On May 11, 1979, the Suffolk County Police Department presented him with a citation for bravery in recognition of his rescue attempt. By that time the results of his examination had been posted and he was a desk sergeant assigned to Sixth Precinct headquarters.

The promotion carried with it a significant increase in salary, and with further help from Maureen's earnings at Kings Park, the Ryans began to catch up on their bills. Michael's migraine headaches returned, however, and his hearing continued to deteriorate. He returned to the Veterans Administration offices and regained his ten percent disability benefits for loss of hearing.

Kerry acquired half a racehorse. Michael's aunt and uncle gave a trotter to their son, Donald, the former helicopter pilot, and he registered it in his name and in Kerry's. The horse was named We Do Fantastic.

Kerry also became the initially reluctant owner of a ten-week-old puppy. It was a beautiful wirehaired Kerry Blue terrier, a breed which generally dislikes other animals but is known for its protective affection toward children. It appeared to be perfect for a child such as Kerry. Her parents had looked for a Kerry Blue for six months, and they drove to the far end of New Jersey to pick it up.

Kerry was terrified of her pet, and her parents and grandparents could do nothing to reassure her the dog wouldn't hurt her. They learned why a few nights later when Kerry asked when the dog was going to take its head off. About two months earlier her Grandmother Ryan and her Aunt Dee, had taken her to a restaurant where a woman wearing a costume of Snoopy from the *Peanuts* comic strip was entertaining children. The costume frightened Kerry, so the woman removed the head to demonstrate there was a person inside.

Confronted with her first puppy a few weeks later, Kerry assumed that someone was in its stomach.

"When is it going to happen?" she asked her mother.

"When is what going to happen?" Maureen asked back.

"When is it going to take its head off?"

Once Kerry's parents knew what the problem was, they talked it over with her. Assured that the dog was not the frightening being she had thought it to be, Kerry and her pet became best friends.

Despite the misunderstanding concerning her puppy, Kerry was displaying a radiant maturity, and except for respiratory infections that continued to plague her, she was in reasonably good health. Outfitted with crutches and heavy braces that cost $1,000 a pair, and which she rapidly outgrew, Kerry was doing limited walking. But most of the time she accepted the faster and easier option of scooting across the floor on her diaper-padded bottom. She was quick and bright, and continuously amazed her family with her frequent knowledge and grasp of ideas generally assumed to be too complex for children her age. She had always shown an incredible resilience, and she had a spirit that couldn't be quashed.

Her carefully nurtured sense of independence continued to be encouraged, although it was sometimes difficult for her parents to draw the fine line between their natural desire to shield her from hurt and overprotectiveness. Love, no matter how heartfelt, could not erase the reality of a lifetime of handicaps.

Not everyone was adjusting to the aftermath of crises as well as the Ryans. A new wave of veterans had returned

home from the first war lost by the United States convinced they hadn't been allowed to win. Their return was
to a country that was humiliated and split in defeat. A
number of the later veterans, unlike most of those who
served in the mid- and late 1960s, were drug abusers and
addicts. Some had taken their habits into the military with
them; others had acquired them there, after exposure to
the cheap, potent marijuana, opium, and heroin so easily
available in Southeast Asia.

The United States had committed approximately 2.6
million men to serve in Vietnam during its involvement
in the war, including 57,000 who died and another
303,000 who were wounded. The last to leave were barely
home before President Jimmy Carter announced on his
second day in office—in January 1977—amnesty for draft
resisters.

People talked of veterans who drank, doped, engaged
in barroom brawls, committed crimes, and who couldn't
or wouldn't hold jobs. Bureaucrats and professionals in
medicine and the social sciences began bandying about
terms like "PVS—Post Vietnam Syndrome." Television
shows regularly depicted Vietnam veterans as madmen,
dope addicts, criminals, baby killers, and suicides. In 1974,
one year after America's complete withdrawal from the
war, a study sponsored by the Veterans Administration
and Department of Defense was completed by a team of
researchers at Washington University in St. Louis. Of
some 600 veterans selected in a random sampling, one in
five had been arrested within six months after their return
from Vietnam.

Most Vietnam veterans were hardly aware of the study
undertaken under the auspices of the DOD, which had
sent them overseas, and the VA, which was supposed to
help them when they returned home. They were through
dealing with the Defense Department, but they were
very much concerned with the failings of the VA.

About half the men wounded in Vietnam had been injured seriously enough to require hospitalization, and about half of those, some 75,000, left the service severely handicapped. Approximately 25,000 are still totally disabled. Many of the wounded survived only because of their almost immediate evacuation from the battlefield by helicopter, and rapid treatment. Consequently many wounded men who would have died in other wars were left alive, but maimed and crippled for life.

Once they were home, most of those who were permanently disabled, or who faced long-term hospitalization, joined thousands of veterans from World War I, World War II, and the Korean War in 171 hospitals, 95 nursing homes and a dozen or more domiciliaries which are part of the VA Department of Medicine and Surgery. There are some three million disabled American veterans, including those who became ill or were injured after military service.

Bobby Muller, paralyzed by a Viet Cong bullet survived, teaching himself to walk with a brace and crutches when he wasn't using a wheelchair. Already a college graduate, he returned to class at Hofstra Law School, earned a law degree, and was married. He eventually moved into a home on Long Island with a specially constructed bathroom, wide corridors, and a car that he drives himself.

Paul Reutershan had no trouble with the law and no immediate problems with the VA when he returned to the United States. His job-seeking persistence finally paid off when he was hired as a train conductor in Connecticut. He was proud of his job and so pleased with the pay and security it offered he began to contemplate marriage. But the severe stomach pains he experienced during the Labor Day weekend in 1977 led him to check into Norwalk Hospital for treatment and tests. Two months later doctors advised him that the pain was caused by terminal cancer. The disease that was eating away at his stomach, colon, and liver was inoperable. Doctors estimated he had between two months and a year to live.

The pronouncement was a death sentence, and he was shattered by the diagnosis. Reutershan couldn't understand why he had been singled out for the disease. His personal habits were exemplary. He didn't smoke or drink, and he ate properly. He was so judicious about his personal habits and physical well-being that friends sometimes referred to him good-naturedly as a health nut. His health should have been excellent. Instead he was dying.

Reutershan began to suspect that his illness might be connected with the clouds of herbicide sprayed over the Vietnamese countryside from C-123s. His helicopter had flown through the sickly sweet mists many times. Within a few weeks, his research had thoroughly convinced him that the chemical was responsible not only for the disease that was killing him, but also for other ailments that were ruining and threatening the lives of thousands of veterans and their children.

Shortly before the end of 1977, with the aide of his sister, Jane Dziedzic, he formed Agent Orange Victims International (AOVI). He also filed a personal damage claim against the government, alleging that his illness was caused by the herbicide he had been exposed to in Vietnam.

Reutershan learned he wasn't alone in his convictions when he talked with a VA counselor in Chicago who had launched an independent study of her own to pin down the connection between the toxic chemical spray and serious health problems among young Vietnam veterans.

Mrs. Maude DeVictor was a thirty-eight-year-old former Navy hospital corpsman who worked in the benefits section of the Chicago Regional Office of the VA. The first time she heard of the existence of the dioxin-tainted herbicide nicknamed Agent Orange occurred when she took a telephone call from the wife of an ill veteran.

The benefits claims counselor had accepted scores of calls from other women anticipating early widowhood, and considered many of the women to be disturbingly "cold and deliberate" about ascertaining the extent of benefits they could expect after the deaths of their husbands. Mrs. Charlie Owens was different.

"This lady called crying. It was just like a teenage love affair," Mrs. DeVictor remembered. "She was calling right from the hospital because the doctors had just told her he was terminally ill and there was nothing they could do but make him comfortable by sedating him. All she knew was that he had told her in healthier days that if his death was ever due to cancer, it was because of the chemicals used in Vietnam."

The thirty-year Air Force veteran who had served during World War II, the Korean War, and the undeclared war in Vietnam, died shortly afterward. And a few months later Mrs. DeVictor learned that the VA had refused the widow's claims for full benefits on grounds that the death was not service related. Mrs. Owens was awarded only a veteran's survivor's pension, some two hundred and seventy-five dollars per month less than if her husband's death had been ruled service-connected.

Mrs. DeVictor was upset at the couple's treatment and intrigued by the possibility of a link between Owens's fatal cancer and the herbicide sprayed in Vietnam. She telephoned the Pentagon and talked with employees at the office of the Judge Advocate General, who advised her the problem was medical, not legal. She was referred to the Air Force Surgeon General's office, and after repeated calls she eventually reached Captain Alvin L. Young,

Ph.D., a plant physiologist and associate professor of life
sciences at the U.S. Air Force Academy.

What is a plant physiologist doing in the Air Force? she
later recalled wondering. They don't have potted plants
on SAC bombers, so why do they need a plant physiologist? It was like having a birth control clinic in a convent.

Gradually Maude DeVictor began to learn about Operation Ranch Hand, and the defoliation and herbicide program in Southeast Asia. An Air Force spokesman attempted to reassure her there was no proven link
between dioxin, the toxic contaminant produced during
the manufacture of the chemical, and cancer.

Mrs. DeVictor is a persistent woman who can be aggressive and courageous when she believes she is right. An
appeal was filed, and compensation was eventually won
for the widow, although the VA refused to concede that
Owens's cancer was caused by his exposure to the herbicide sprayed in Vietnam.

Mrs. DeVictor had been a premedical student at Ripon
College in Wisconsin before enlisting in the Navy. After
talking with Mrs. Owens, Mrs. DeVictor spent some time
during the Christmas holiday season at a VA hospital,
where she found a number of young Vietnam veterans ill
with forms of cancer she knew to be unusual in persons
of their age. She began assembling statistics from widows
of young Vietnam veterans who had died of cancer and
polled ex-servicemen who came into the VA office, asking
if they were ever troubled with a severe acnelike rash.
She also asked them if they had frequent headaches. Did
they undergo frequent changes of mood or flashes of temper? Had they experienced a loss of sex drive? Had their
wives had miscarriages, stillbirths, or given birth to deformed children?

Those who responded affirmatively to a majority of the
questions inevitably shared at least two other things in

common. They had been in Vietnam, and they had been in areas sprayed with herbicides.

By early 1978 Mrs. DeVictor had assembled more than fifty case histories of veterans exposed to Agent Orange who had developed or died of cancer, suffered from chloracne or other maladies commonly associated with dioxin exposure, or who had wives who suffered miscarriages or gave birth to children with congenital defects. A ghastly pattern to the physical and psychiatric disorders of veterans and of their families had taken shape. And it pointed to a disturbing link with exposure to herbicides sprayed in Vietnam. When Mrs. DeVictor approached her superiors with the information, she says, she was ordered to discontinue collecting the data.

Although no one in a position of authority admitted as much, the implications of Mrs. DeVictor's research were staggering. If the VA conceded that Owens's fatal cancer —or the maladies affecting other veterans, their wives, or children—were linked with Agent Orange, a precedent could be established that would open the way for tens of thousands of damage suits against the government and chemical manufacturers.

Mrs. DeVictor suspected, furthermore, that official recognition of Agent Orange claims might also open the door to reparations to victims in Vietnam and eventually lead to international charges against the United States of committing crimes against humanity.

The determined VA employee went public. She shared her information with Ron DeYoung, a veterans' counselor at Columbia College on the south edge of Chicago's Loop. He had telephoned to verify data on the school application of a veteran when she asked if he knew anything about "fogging," the chemical spraying of vegetation in Vietnam. DeYoung knew hardly anything about the project.

But he worked at a college known for its strong communications program, and he indicated he had contacts with people who could help Mrs. DeVictor carry the story of her suspicions to the public. They talked by phone for half an hour, and when Mrs. DeVictor left work that afternoon, she walked to DeYoung's office at the college and they talked and studied the reports, government memos, letters, and other documentation she had collected for two more hours.

DeYoung took the information to one of the college instructors who was affiliated with WBBM-TV, Chicago's CBS outlet. News anchorman Bill Kurtis, working with Rose Economu and Brian Boyer, responded by preparing an hour-long documentary called "Agent Orange, the Deadly Fog," which was broadcast on March 23, 1978. Veterans, VA spokesmen, and scientists including the Air Force's Captain Young were interviewed and appeared in the documentary. One of the most dramatic and disturbing features of the program was film clips of deformed Vietnamese babies born to parents exposed to the herbicidal spray. References were made to Dr. Ton That Tung's work, and it was noted that his early reports on the possible carcinogenic and teratogenic effects of the herbicide had been labeled propaganda by American military and political leaders.

The morning after the broadcast, Mrs. DeVictor's office at the VA was besieged with telephone calls from journalists, veterans, and government officials. She wasn't permitted to take the calls, and after a period of tense confrontation, the woman who had taken the first step in the crusade that would earn her a sobriquet as "the mother of the Agent Orange movement" was transferred to another, presumably less sensitive, department.

Mrs. DeVictor nevertheless continued loudly to spread her Cassandra warning about Agent Orange wherever she could find a forum, and unofficially to counsel worried veterans or their wives by mail and by phone. Her telephone bills soared, and letters and cards found their way to her Southside Chicago apartment by the score, despite incomplete addresses and frequent misspellings.

It was no surprise that her relationship with her supervisors at the VA offices deteriorated. Other employees also began avoiding her, apparently fearful of being seen in her company. She was passed over for promotion, her work evaluation marks dipped, and she was involved in one skirmish after another at work until she finally walked off the job early in 1981.

She had been operated on for breast cancer in 1976, followed by two years of chemotherapy, and she angrily charged that she was forced to quit her job at the VA to protect her health after being assigned to a desk next to a video display terminal (VDT). Used in many daily newspaper newsrooms, VDTs emit low level radiation and have been a source of controversy over charges that they can cause, or aggravate, cancer, as well as lead to eyestrain and a variety of other ills.

Mrs. DeVictor also filed a personal claim against the U.S. Navy, alleging that she was contaminated with radiation while working at the Philadelphia Naval Hospital as a corpsman between 1959 and 1961. She claimed the damage occurred while she was using radium pellets in an experimental chemotherapy program treating women with uterine cancer.

During the summer of 1978, Mrs. DeVictor had accepted a phone call from an ABC-TV network executive in New York who told her about a veteran who had walked into the studios and announced that he was dying of cancer caused by his exposure to chemical spray in Vietnam. The spokesman said that the veteran claimed she could verify his story. ABC wanted to confirm the information. Mrs. DeVictor said the young man was probably right, and told them about her research. Before concluding the conversation, she asked for the veteran's name and phone number. That night she telephoned Paul Reutershan, and they talked for an hour.

Reutershan used his remaining days of life to alert others about the danger of Agent Orange and to persuade Congress, government agencies, and the chemical industry to uncover the truth about it. He was determined to force the VA and the DOD into an admission that dioxin poisoning stemming from the spraying program was the cause of many of the ailments afflicting Vietnam veterans and their issue. The dying veteran utilized television and radio shows to spread his message. It was always the same: "Agent Orange is a killer."

Reutershan appeared on NBC television's *Today Show*, but left the studio disconsolate after what he perceived to be the open skepticism of interviewer Jane Pauley. But other members of the media were anxious to listen and to provide a forum for the determined young veteran. He appeared on cable TV in New York and on other national television and radio programs, and gave numerous newspaper interviews.

On December 14, 1978, Paul Reutershan died in the Norwalk, Connecticut, hospital; he was twenty-eight. He was still trying to prove that the malignancy that had destroyed his body had been caused by dioxin in the chemicals his helicopter flew through in Vietnam. The day he died, a check arrived from the VA, acknowledging that his health problems were service connected. Significantly, however, there was no admission that the cancer was caused by exposure to Agent Orange. Reutershan was too weak to sign the check when it finally arrived, and two days after his death his family received a notice from the VA demanding its return. It was returned that day.

A few weeks after the young veteran's death, both ABC-TV's *20/20* and the Public Broadcasting Corporation's *For Your Information* featured Agent Orange in programs that were televised nationally.

After the death of Reutershan, the torch passed to Frank McCarthy, an energetic and resolute disabled Vietnam veteran. McCarthy had worked with other disabled Vietnam veterans before he met Reutershan and acceded to a deathbed plea to assume the presidency of the AOVI and carry on its work. The two men knew each other for only a short time, but it was long enough for McCarthy to develop a healthy respect both for the dying man and his work. Years later McCarthy still remembered Reutershan "taking telephone calls from worried veterans while he was in his hospital bed. He did it until the day he died." McCarthy, who first heard of Reutershan when he saw the ailing veteran being interviewed on a television show, now leads the crusade from his apartment in Manhattan. Reutershan's sister, Mrs. Jane Dziedzic, and his mother, Muriel, as AOVI secretary and treasurer respectively, give almost full time to the effort to inform worried veterans about Agent Orange, and to lobbying for recognition of the part played by the government and the chemical manufacturers in the poisoning of Vietnam veterans, and for changes in VA policy.

Claims for disability benefits or treatment by Vietnam veterans who cited ailments to themselves or to their children as a result of exposure to Agent Orange were still trickling into the VA. And they were still summarily denied. There was no documented evidence that the troubles were service related, the VA continued to insist.

Maureen Ryan began to suspect as early as 1976 that Kerry's birth defects and Michael's health problems were

somehow tied to his exposure to Agent Orange. Maureen
was reading a health magazine one day when she discovered a short article mentioning a possible link between
Agent Orange and the medical problems of veterans and
their children. Her interest was piqued, and she soon
began noticing other references to Agent Orange in
magazines and newspapers.

By 1978 Maureen was investigating her suspicions in
earnest. She learned about dioxin, the worst and most
terrible of dozens of contaminants unavoidably created as
by-products during the manufacturing process for
phenoxy herbicides. Dioxin is formed when trichlophenol
and similar compounds are heated to high temperatures.
It can be absorbed through the skin, as well as ingested
through water or food.

Dioxin is not water soluble. It has a half-life in water of
approximately thirty years, meaning that after three
decades, it is still half as toxic as it was when it was formed.
Thousands of American servicemen in Vietnam caught
runoff rainwater from tents and other structures as Michael did, or scooped it up in canteens and helmets from
streams and rivers to drink it. There is an excellent possibility that the water was contaminated with some of the
tons of Agent Orange, Agent Blue, Agent White, or Agent
Purple the American military dumped over the rain forests and rice fields of Vietnam. Soldiers drank and washed
in the water that was available to them. The cautious ones
dropped in water purification tablets first, then waited the
half hour recommended in training manuals before drinking.

Maureen learned about chloracne, the skin disorder
that so closely resembled the angry pus-filled sores that
sometimes broke out on Michael's legs and thighs and
behind his ears. She learned that the lumps can also appear on the groin, genitals, buttocks, and face, fill with oily

blackheads, swell as big as dimes, and burst, leaving horrible scars. And she learned that the rash is the primary symptom of dioxin poisoning.

She also learned that other symptoms, documented after various instances of accidental exposure, include liver diseases, intolerance to alcohol, headaches, psychiatric and nervous system disorders, reduction of sex drive, fatigue, loss of sensation in the extremities, changes in skin tone and sensitivity to light.

Her discovery of the teratogenic and mutagenic effect of dioxin on fetuses was even more disturbing. Dioxin has been described as "the defiler of wombs." Maureen read of the charges made by Dr. Ton That Tung, and she read of the women in Vietnam who miscarried or who gave birth to pitifully deformed infants. She remembered one of the things Michael's mother had said to her shortly after Kerry's birth, while doctors were still discovering one abnormality after another: "I've seen babies with everything wrong: trouble with the cardiovascular system, the bones, intestines, genital-urinary system, the brain. . . . But Kerry doesn't have your run-of-the-mill abnormalities. There had to be a massive insult to the embryo from the outside."

There was hardly any doubt left in Maureen's mind that her family's health had been sacrificed to the dreadful contaminant in the chemical spray used in Vietnam. Michael's illnesses and Kerry's deformities dovetailed with what Maureen had learned of dioxin exposure. She began to tell her friends at work about the deadly herbicidal spray, the magazine and newspaper articles she was reading, and about what she was learning from the books dealing with chemicals and genetics that she borrowed from the public library. It was obvious that they didn't believe her. They thought she was looking for an excuse for Kerry's imperfect body.

The only person it was important for Maureen to convince, however, was her cynical policeman husband. And she put together an impressive collection of documentation to do the job. If there had been even a shred of doubt left in her mind, it was dissipated after she talked with Michael's cousin, Donald, one day after he had driven from the U.S. Army Military Academy at West Point, where he was assigned, to Stony Brook for a visit. She was sitting at the kitchen table surrounded by her books and magazine clippings when he walked inside to help himself to a cup of coffee. She knew that he was knowledgeable about chemicals and had flown on spray missions.

Maureen asked him if Michael had been in defoliated areas of Vietnam. Donald's affirmative reply provided the final link she needed. Her suspicions about the tie between Agent Orange and her family's health were confirmed.

Despite his wife's certainty, as a policeman Michael had been trained to demand incontrovertible proof and always to be suspicious in the absence of hard evidence. He was interested, but skeptical. He had also formed an unpleasant stereotype in his mind about some of the young veterans groups like the Vietnam Veterans Against the War. He didn't like the image he felt they projected of long-haired hippies, and street radicals who could be manipulated like so many sheep by a handful of hardcore left wingers.

But he listened, and he thought about the information Maureen had accumulated. The statistics, facts, and case histories amounted to an argument that was difficult to ignore. She counted off the symptoms of dioxin poisoning: chloracne, sudden weight loss, migraine headaches, insomnia, intolerance to alcohol, birth defects, and hearing impairment. The symptoms were all disturbingly familiar to both husband and wife. Michael's hearing loss may not have been caused simply by the concussion from the mortar blast after all, Maureen argued. Michael began to think about Agent Orange and his wife's insistence that it was at the root of the family's health problems.

One night in late December 1978, Maureen was reading a newspaper while Michael was putting on his uniform and preparing to go to work. She noticed a column by Jimmy Breslin, in which the writer told of the death of Paul Reutershan, the young veteran whose name she had been seeing in articles about the chemical spray used in Vietnam. Reutershan was quoted as complaining that he should have been told that he had been issued a death sentence when he was ordered to Vietnam.

The magnitude of Reutershan's death swept over her. She realized that his life had been stolen from him. She turned and peered at Kerry, who was sitting nearby in her wheelchair. Maureen didn't need any more information to convince her of the perniciousness of the chemicals her husband had been exposed to. Reutershan's death and her daughter's damaged body were proof enough. Her face flushed with anger. Then she began to cry.

Michael was puzzled by the tears. He couldn't understand how she could become so distressed over someone she had never met. Maureen had stopped crying before he left the house, and she told him that she was going to call a lawyer who was said to have information about the chemical spray used in Vietnam.

An hour later Michael answered the telephone at the Sixth Precinct and the man at the other end of the line identified himself as Victor Yannacone, an attorney from the Long Island community of Patchogue. Yannacone said he thought it would be a good idea if they met and talked about Agent Orange. He drove to the station that night, gave Michael a copy of a 163-page brief of a class-action lawsuit he had prepared on behalf of veterans and their families who were suffering from the effects of exposure to Agent Orange, and began to talk. After work the men met and talked for six hours about Vietnam, dying veterans, congenitally deformed babies, and Agent Orange. After Yannacone left, Michael studied the brief for another hour.

When he drove home, there was no longer any doubt in his mind that his wife was right. The sudden weight loss he had undergone while he was a New York City policeman had released dioxin that had been stored like a chemical time bomb in his body fat, back into his system. Kerry's carefully planned conception had occurred at one of the worst possible times.

The herbicide sprayed so casually in Vietnam killed—and it crippled babies. Perhaps most infuriating of all, Michael realized: The government had known!

7

DIOXIN'S DEADLY LEGACY

Maureen was slipping into a jacket and preparing to leave for work when Michael walked into the house. His face was pale and his mouth was creased into a thin line as he reached out his hand and pushed the legal brief at her.

"I don't care what goes on at work today, I want you to take the time to read this brief," he said. "A couple of times."

That afternoon he picked her up at work, and the first thing she said as she slid into the car seat beside him was, "Michael, they knew about it."

The revelation was shattering. They had been raised to trust in their government and in their country. The sense of betrayal when they considered the magnitude of the injury and the wrong done to them was enormous. They felt as though the chemical companies who manufactured the poison and the generals in the Pentagon who permitted its use had broken into their home and deliberately mutilated their child. The grief and pain of the past eight years swept over them in a wave.

Discovery that Michael's exposure to an outside chemical agent in Vietnam was responsible for Kerry's troubled birth brought the pain back all over again. Mick Ryan had been right all along. God wasn't responsible for Kerry's maimed body; it was the American chemical industry and the Department of Defense.

Maureen found herself looking at her daughter and seeing the birth defects. Previously it was Kerry she noticed, not her physically imperfect body. When Maureen knelt on the floor to change her eight-year-old daughter's diaper, she was filled with hate for the bureaucrats and the generals who were responsible for the indignity Kerry had to endure. Kerry's birth hadn't extracted as severe an emotional toll on her parents as their belated realization of betrayal—and of what might have been.

Because of corporate greed and government callousness, Kerry would never have a brother or sister. Now that the family knew the real reason behind their troubles, it was obvious that Michael and Maureen could not take the chance of becoming parents to another child so severely handicapped.

The dioxin that seeped so insidiously into Michael's system in Vietnam may have damaged his chromosomes so drastically that he can never again hope to father a healthy child. Or it may have accumulated in his body fat to await release at any time to wreak destruction to his system or his unborn child's. No one knows the exact extent of the danger.

Michael's sisters had married brothers who were each Vietnam veterans, and both had been in areas exposed to the treacherous chemical spray that was proving so deadly to plant life, soldiers, and the unborn. The young couples postponed plans for beginning families.

Ironically the revelation that was so emotionally devastating to Kerry's parents, lifted a psychic weight from her tiny shoulders. It had been difficult for her to understand why she was not as healthy and physically able as others around her, and she was troubled with vague feelings of guilt. But comprehension and comfort accompanied knowledge that an outside force was responsible. She no longer had any doubt that her condition was not her fault.

One night sometime after her parents began talking about Agent Orange and such esoteric subjects as carcinogens, mutagens, teratogens, and dioxin, they noticed her busily scribbling on several sheets of lined notebook paper.

"What are you doing, Kerry?" her father asked.

"I'm writing a book," she replied, leaning closer to the paper and frowning in concentration.

"A book? About what?"

"About Agent Orange. About how the bad men sprayed you and hurt me," she said.

Michael was frustrated when he thought of the alternatives that would have been available to himself and his wife had they known of the dangers to their unborn child. He could have maintained his weight until the child was conceived, continuing to store the chemical toxin in his fatty tissue instead of releasing it into his system at exactly the right time for it to ensure the maximum harm to the developing fetus. Maureen could have undergone sonargrams, the taking of sound pictures of the uterus and fetus, or the analysis of fluid taken from the uterus, to determine if the baby she was carrying was whole. They could have adopted a child.

"Dammit," Michael growled, "they sent me a letter in a hurry when they wanted to draft me into the Army. But it's been more than ten years since I got out, and I'm still waiting for a letter telling me I was exposed to a destructive chemical in Vietnam."

Despite the government's reluctance to provide veterans and their families with information about the chemical and its toxic by-product, the data were readily available elsewhere. Dioxin has burned a terrible path through human history ever since the development of chlorinated hydrocarbons nearly forty years ago.

Scientists working initially at the University of Chicago and later at the Biological Warfare Research Center at Camp (later Fort) Detrick, Maryland, developed herbicides near the end of World War II. They were considered for use on at least a small scale in the Pacific, but the emergence of the atomic bomb ended the war before they could be employed by American forces.

The United States had taken a leading role at the 1925 Geneva Convention drafting the Geneva Protocol banning bacteriological agents and gases in warfare. But although the treaty was signed by the U.S., it was never ratified by the Senate. And although the American government has continued to claim it agrees with the protocol, not being a signatory, it is not legally bound by the code. The U.S. consistently insists on classifying its herbicides as defoliants, and maintains that defoliation does not constitute chemical warfare.

In 1972 both the U.S. and the Soviet Union signed the Convention on the Prohibition of the Development, Production, and Stockpiling of Bacteriological and Toxic Weapons. But neither super power agreed to ban chemical weapons, and both are known to have huge stockpiles of gases in their arsenals, especially incapacitating elements such as tear gas, and poison gases destructive to the nervous system.

Both the United Nations and the World Health Organization have denounced use of the chemical agents in Southeast Asia. And the WHO specifically criticized American use of tear gas and defoliants, pointing out that the latter was strongly suspected of causing birth abnormalities.

Field tests on the compounds developed during World War II, including the two most powerful herbicides, 2,4-D and 2,4,5-T, were conducted in Puerto Rico, in Texas and at Fort Drum, N.Y. The first recorded military application occurred in the '50s, when the British sprayed 2,4,5-T along communication routes while fighting Communist insurgents in Malaysia.

The first large-scale testing and use of herbicides in the civil war in Vietnam occurred in 1961, when Michael Ryan was a sixteen-year-old senior at Midwood High School in Brooklyn, and Maureen O'Connor was a fifteen-year-old student at St. Helen's in the Bronx. A few months later, in February 1962, President John F. Kennedy announced that U.S. military advisers in Vietnam were authorized to protect themselves by returning fire if fired upon by the Viet Cong.

American scientists from plant science laboratories at Camp Detrick, the U.S. Department of Agriculture, and the U.S. Forest Service studied the Southeast Asian countryside to determine which defoliants and herbicides would be most effective on the indigenous plant life. Some two-thirds of the land was covered with dense forests and jungles, and a spraying program was considered to be the best method of destroying selective areas that provided cover for the enemy.

Highways were the initial targets of the American chemical attacks on the Vietnamese ecosystem, and U.S. forces resisted initial requests by their allies to spray enemy food crops. Before the end of the year, however, American military advisers were teaching South Vietnamese pilots how to do their own spraying and destroy rice, manioc, sweet potatoes, and other food crops in areas controlled by the Viet Cong. By 1964 American pilots were applying defoliants in nearby Thailand in support of combat operations against Thai insurgents.

On the home front the chemical technology developed during World War II had left the United States and the rest of the world with access to a brilliantly promising arsenal of new weapons with which to protect its food crops, forests, and rangelands by controlling insect pests and regulating plant growth. The most wondrous and best-known chemical armament of all was DDT, but there were other chlorinated hydrocarbons like endrine, heptachlor, chlordane, and dieldrin, as well as 2,4,5-T and 2,4-D. All were chlorinated hydrocarbons. By the 1950s the phosphates were developed and the U.S. Department of Agriculture, as well as individual farmers, ranchers and foresters were almost completely won over to chemical control of pests and plants. The chemicals enabled farmers to record incredible increases in their crop yields, foresters to eliminate unwanted brush and tree species, and homeowners to rid their lawns of pesky crabgrass and dandelions.

Domestic use of 2,4-dichlorophenoxy-acetic acid (2,4-D), one of the components of Agent Orange, was well advanced during the early postwar years clearing plant growth along highways, the right-of-way of railroads and power lines, weeds from rice fields, and brush from rangeland.

It wasn't until the early '60s, that Rachel Carson's eloquent warning in her frightening book *Silent Spring* caused people and government agencies to begin to take a second, serious look at the chemical revolution in agriculture. Led by biologists and a few other perceptive scientists, critics of plant-growth regulators and insect sprays began to spread the word about devastation of wildlife and the infiltration of poisons into the human food chain through contaminated plants and animals caused by reckless chemical use. And ironically the insect pests that were the initial targets of much of the chemical assault began developing resistance. Even DDT was losing its lethal effect on insect pests, although its toxicity didn't appear to lessen for other forms of animal life.

The age of chemistry born in the 1940s had nevertheless ushered in a powerful new profitmaking industry in
the United States that was doing an international business
thirty-five years later exceeding $100 billion annually. In
addition to some 43,000 different chemicals and 40,000
pesticides, the industry was turning out plastics, drugs,
synthetic fabrics, and a host of other modern products
that consumers were quickly convinced they couldn't do
without.

The first-known serious industrial accident involving
2,4,5-T occurred in 1949, when an explosion blew the lid
off a vat where the chemical was brewing at a plant
owned by the Monsanto Corporation in Nitro, West Virginia. A thick coating of brown dust tainted with 2,4,5-T's
inevitable contaminant, dioxin, settled through the building. Members of the cleanup crews and other employees
who were exposed to the toxic mess became sick. Eventually 228 people developed chloracne, the distinctive
symptom of dioxin poisoning. Then workers began to
complain about a host of other puzzling health problems, some as ominous as skin cancer, others as difficult
to pin down as chronic fatigue and nervousness. Investigative studies commissioned both by Monsanto and
by the United Steelworkers of America proved inconclusive.

By 1953 male employees at the plant owned by Ba-
discher Anilin & Soda-Fabrik, a manufacturer of 2,4,5-T
in Ludwigshaften am Rhein, Germany, as well as their
wives, children, and pets, began developing chloracne.
Traces of the chemical were being carried home on the
clothing and bodies of the employees.

A few months after the appearance of the chloracne
was first noticed, an explosion also occurred in the
B.A.S.F. plant, and subsequent medical examinations of
the employees turned up a host of ailments now known

to be symptomatic of dioxin exposure. Workers had liver damage, heart trouble, and heightened blood pressure. Some proved to be bothered by fits of depression, memory loss, and difficulty concentrating.

Five years after the accident a worker was assigned to work near the reactor, or cooking vat, involved in the explosion. Although he wore protective clothing, he removed his face mask several times during his shift, and four days later he broke out in a nasty rash, was complaining of headaches and difficulty in hearing. Nine months later, after developing pancreatitis and an upper-abdominal tumor, he was dead. Another employee worked on the reactor for two hours. He developed chloracne, a spot on his lungs, became psychotic, and five years later committed suicide.

Dutch workers were contaminated with dioxin in 1963, when an explosion occurred in a factory manufacturing 2,4,5-T in Amsterdam. A decade after the explosion the plant was determined to be still so dangerously contaminated with dioxin that it was dismantled, imbedded in concrete, and buried at sea.

By 1964 the Dow Chemical Company, which would become the largest American manufacturer of Agent Orange, disclosed that more than seventy of its employees at a plant in Midland, Michigan, which produced 2,4,5-T, were experiencing an outbreak of chloracne. Dr. Benjamin Holder, at that time director of Dow's Midland Division, described the symptoms as including fatigue, lassitude, depression, skin eruptions, and weight loss.

Dow conducted an independent study involving 220 workers with various amounts of exposure to 2,4,5-T and to 2,4-D and 4,600 individuals as controls. After examination of the men studied, no differences were reported between the study group and the controls.

Additional tests were conducted on small animals, using

various doses of dioxin. Dioxin itself was determined to be one of the most toxic substances known.

Other instances of workers accidentally exposed to 2,4-D and 2,4,5-T have occurred in Czechoslovakia, Poland, and England, but the world's worst and most widely publicized chemical manufacturing mishap occurred at Seveso, Italy, a town of 17,000 north of Milan, on June 10, 1976. An explosion ripped through the huge Icmesa Chemical works, rupturing pipes and releasing a poisonous cloud of residue that showered the farming and manufacturing community with dioxin.* Thirteen days later 739 residents of Seveso and smaller communities nearby were evacuated.

By that time, animals had begun to die, and the bodies of children had broken out in ugly blackheads and pus-filled sores. Some 270 acres of the most severely contaminated property were sealed off with an eight-foot-high plastic fence. Armed guards wearing protective clothing, including masks over their mouths and noses, were posted to prevent access to the contaminated farms, homes, schools, and businesses isolated inside. Seveso was an environmental disaster.

Thousands of dogs, cats, chickens, rabbits, birds, and other small animals were dead after having eaten vegetables, grains, and other food coated with dioxin. Eventually the animal toll, including some slaughtered because of suspected contamination, reached 87,000. The animals, clothing, and household possessions of the evacuees were sealed in drums and underground silos. Topsoil from the most virulently contaminated area was removed to a depth of eight inches by workers wearing protective

---

*The chemical being manufactured when the explosion occurred was not 2,4,5-T, but hexachloraphene, an antibacterial formerly used in such everyday substances as soap and toothpaste.

clothing after disclosure that the dioxin had seeped into the earth.

Authorities eventually reported that 187 people, including a disproportionately large number of children, had broken out with chloracne. One of the most seriously affected was three-year-old Alicia Senno, whose terribly scarred body was shown in a news photo circulated around the world.

A year after the accident the Italian government had documented thirty-eight cases of birth defects in the area. By 1978 the number had burgeoned to fifty-three. There had been only four in 1976. Yet, according to the town's mayor, none of the fetal abnormalities observed in 1977 and 1978 involved major deformities. There were none of the "monster" births that residents were led to fear. Other women suffered miscarriages and stillbirths, but after official warnings cautioning about the danger of genetic damage to fetuses, the birth rate dropped precipitously. More than thirty women applied for legal and religious permission to abort.

The political and emotional aftermath of the industrial disaster was widespread and extreme. Construction of at least one chemical plant in Sicily was temporarily halted, and action groups launched bitter campaigns to halt still other building projects they considered to be potentially dangerous to the environment. Demands were pressed before legislators and other government officials for installation of costly antipollution equipment by industries and for closer adherence to safety regulations.

American biologist and environmentalist Barry Commoner had been scheduled to lecture in Italy a short time after the accident occurred, and he was invited to assist in the investigation. Commoner donned protective clothing and entered the most severely contaminated zone a few weeks after it was evacuated.

He was later quoted as speculating whether it would be better to decontaminate by removing a foot of topsoil and incinerate it at extremely high temperatures to destroy the dioxin and somehow clean up the houses, or to seal off the zone and keep it as a grim shrine to the petrochemical industry.*

Even with the decision to decontaminate, carrying out the plan posed incredible difficulties. Huge mounds of topsoil, vegetation, household, and other personal belongings, as well as animal carcasses, had to be decontaminated or destroyed. Dioxin is a stable substance which doesn't rapidly degrade despite claims by the chemical industry that tests have proven it is destroyed by sunlight. Environmentalists counter with their own research, which they insist indicates that it may remain toxic for up to thirty years before it is destroyed by the action of bacteria in the soil. While Agent Orange was still in use in Vietnam, they say, even government research indicated that it remained active in the environment for at least fourteen years.

Officials of F. Hoffman & Co., the Swiss drug and chemical giant that owned the plant, suggested burying the contaminated material underneath the town in cement ossuaries lined with charcoal. Others alternatively suggested that gamma radiation might be used to break down the molecules in dioxin, that it be loaded in drums and dumped in the ocean, or buried in an abandoned German coal mine. Frustrated government officials finally had Seveso's contaminated topsoil, dead animals, and other materials bagged and stored in a vacant school building in the abandoned area to await final resolution of the controversy.

People, June 11, 1979.

The chemical company meanwhile voluntarily spent $25 million for cleanup and compensation to victims sickened or chased from their homes by the disaster. By late 1979 most of the evacuated residents had returned to their homes, and spokesmen for the government and the company announced that an out-of-court settlement providing compensation to victims and repayment of expenses incurred by governmental agencies were agreed upon. Separate statements issued by the two parties disagreed on the amount of money involved, it was reported. The government said the company agreed to pay $114 million. A company statement issued in Geneva set the amount at less than half of that, $52 million.

The attention of environmentalists was focused on the United States in 1978 when the New York State Health Department declared a health emergency in the Love Canal neighborhood of Niagara Falls. The state purchased 235 homes of families there after investigation disclosed a possible link between unusually severe and widespread health problems among residents and toxic chemical waste dumped there years earlier.

The Hooker Chemical and Plastics Corporation dumped the waste materials between 1942 and 1953 before selling the property to the Niagara Falls Board of Education for one dollar, with a stipulation that the company would not be held responsible for problems that might occur as a result of the chemicals dumped there. A school and playground were ultimately constructed atop the buried chemicals, and the remaining property was sold to real-estate developers who constructed moderately priced homes.

By the late '70s residents of the neighborhood located over a mile-long trench dug in the late nineteenth century as part of an unsuccessful industrial project, then filled in fifty years later with tons of hazardous chemical waste, were beginning to wonder about the health problems that were so suddenly plaguing them. Children came home from the school playground with strange, inexplicable burns on their arms and legs. Infants in the neighborhood were born mentally retarded or with a host of physical defects. Other pregnancies ended in miscarriages or stillbirths. Of sixteen pregnancies reported in the Love Canal in 1979, apparently only one birth was normal. Pets mysteriously sickened and lost huge clumps of their fur. One woman with cancer began counting her neighbors with various forms of the disease. There were eight.

Many of the health problems reported by the people living in the Love Canal area were disturbingly similar to those caused elsewhere by dioxin.

Investigators learned that chemical waste from the old dump under the school was oozing out of its metal containers and invading back yards and basements and collecting in noxious puddles around the foundations of houses.

Some of the waste was identified as trichlorophenol, a chemical substance closely related to 2,4,5-T, and it was estimated that the ground water at Love Canal held as much as 141 pounds of dioxin. Documents released by a Congressional subcommittee disclosed that Hooker was aware long before the trouble surfaced, that the chemical waste could imperil public health.

In 1980 another health emergency in the Love Canal area was declared by U.S. President Jimmy Carter, and more than 700 additional homes were evacuated. At almost the same time, officials of the U.S. Environmental Protection Agency (EPA) announced that a medical study of thirty-six residents from the chemical dump area disclosed that eleven had aberrations in chromosomes.

The Love Canal had become America's Seveso. But there have been other chemical tragedies in the United States, other miscalculations and accidents. One finally led to a ban on use of Agent Orange in the United States.

In April 1978 the EPA received a letter from an Alsea, Oregon, woman complaining that she and seven neighbors had experienced a total of eleven miscarriages in five years and she believed there might be a link with aerial spraying of the surrounding forests with 2,4,5-T. Could it be, Mrs. Bonnie Hill asked, that the spray which sometimes drifted over her tiny community was responsible for causing the women to abort?

Reacting with surprising alacrity for a government agency, the EPA launched an investigation. A study was commissioned, to be conducted by the Environmental Health Institute of Colorado State University and the University of Miami Medical School Department of Public Health.

The rate of miscarriages per 1,000 live births in Alsea was compared with control areas where there was no spraying, the nearby communities of Eugene and Corvallis, and a heavily forested area similar to Alsea in the eastern portion of the state. The comparisons disclosed that during the month of June through the previous six years, Alsea women experienced 130 miscarriages per 1,000 live births, while Eugene and Corvallis registered forty-four and nine tenths combined, and the forested area in the east showed forty-six. The month of June, eight to twelve weeks after the annual spring spraying of timberland to kill off hardwood trees that compete with the more desirable conifers for space and light, was the peak month for miscarriages in Alsea.

Apprised of the alarming results of the study, EPA

Chief Douglas M. Costle signed an emergency order on February 28, 1979, temporarily suspending the use in the United States of all products containing 2,4,5-T in forests, along rights of way, in pastures, or in the vicinity of homes, aquatic and recreation areas.

The EPA prohibition on the domestic use of 2,4,5-T occurred nearly nine years after the spraying was halted in Vietnam, and was restricted in this country to commercial use by the U.S. Forest Service, timber companies, and other major landowners because of the mounting evidence of its deleterious effect on human and animal life. In 1970 the Department of Agriculture had prohibited the use of 2,4,5-T around homes, recreational sites, and wherever water contamination was likely, and the fledgling EPA attempted to impose a more wide-ranging ban on the suspect herbicide. But after four years of litigation initiated by chemical manufacturers, the EPA was forced to rescind its order. In the meantime the courts had permitted the manufacturers to continue production while the issue was being decided.

Consequently some twelve million acres in the U.S. were treated with the herbicide during nearly a decade between the halt in military use in Vietnam and the new EPA order in 1979. But even the new order represented only a partial ban. Agency spokesmen explained that use of herbicides containing 2,4,5-T was still permitted on the country's extensive rice crops and on rangeland because those uses were not believed to involve significant human exposure. The exclusion of rangeland from the order ignored studies that have detected the presence of dioxin in beef raised in the Midwest.

The timing of the order added to the impact. The ban was invoked virtually at the beginning of the March-April spraying season and halted the anticipated use of an estimated seven million pounds of 2,4,5-T. If the planned spring spraying had been permitted to proceed, some four million people would have been exposed to the chemical, the EPA spokesman claimed.

Supported by angered farmers, foresters, and ranchers, one week after the ban was imposed Dow filed a motion in Federal District Court in Bay City, Michigan, requesting a stay of the emergency order. The National Forest Products Association and scientists at Oregon State University complained that there were statistical errors in the Alsea study. Dow conceded that 2,4,5-T with its contaminant dioxin had been shown to cause cancer in laboratory animals, but there is "no good solid medical evidence," company spokesmen insisted, that the herbicide had the same effect on humans. Dow manufactured more than half of the 2,4,5-T produced in the United States at the time the EPA order was issued. Vertac, the Thompson Hayward Chemical Company, and Rhodia, Inc., were other manufacturers of the herbicides in question.

Judge James Harvey ruled against the chemical company on April 12, 1979, absolving the EPA of any "error of judgment" in claiming that 2,4,5-T was linked to spontaneous abortion in humans.

There have been scores of studies, and some 30,000 to 40,000 scientific papers are believed to have been written on 2,4,5-T, as well as thousands of others on 2,4-D and its cousins. Yet forces on both sides of the controversy continue to accuse each other of not having the scientific evidence to back up its claims. Meanwhile veterans are sick and dying. And their children are being born with terrible birth defects.

8

MOBILIZATION

MEMORIAL

What memorial can we build for the honored
dead more fitting than one which serves the living?
Our veterans grow old and they are alone.
Our veterans are disabled and we do not
care for, or about them.
Our veterans are unemployed and we can not
find jobs for them.
Our veterans are dying and we research it.
Honor is a word out of vogue in this country,
but it is one which we need to address.
In the end, this is our Nation, our country.
In its name, we served and our friends and
families died. Yet, it is this same Nation
which now gives empty ceremony and rhetoric to
the dead and counts the living among the dead.

JOAN MAIMAN, Chairman
Veterans Leadership Conference

It was difficult and painful for the Ryans to deal with their outrage. For the first time—after so many years of distress—they were in a situation they weren't certain they could handle. The anger and hatred were so intense they could barely cope with it.

Victor Yannacone introduced the Ryans to Frank McCarthy. They met at a restaurant to talk, and McCarthy told them about the recently formed Agent Orange Victims International. At that time, the organization's small membership included only McCarthy, Reutershan's mother and sister, and a handful of other people.

Active involvement in the AOVI was important and necessary to the Ryans and to the movement; it provided a positive outlet for them to work off their outrage and depression. And the young organization was in need of dedicated, articulate, and irate volunteers who could become spokesmen for veterans and families who were known victims or potential victims of the insidious toxin brought home from Vietnam in the bodies of GIs.

Frank McCarthy is a slender man of five feet eight inches and 140 pounds of gritty determination and tightly coiled energy. He was operating the AOVI out of his back pocket and the pockets of Reutershan's mother and sister. The organization was $19,000 in debt when McCarthy took over, and the red ink continued to keep pace with the burgeoning membership.

McCarthy had been in tight spots before. Serving with the Army's "Big Red One," the First Infantry Division, in Vietnam's notorious Iron Triangle, his small stature and scrappy spirit led to his selection as a "tunnel rat." The Iron Triangle was an NVA stronghold that was honeycombed with tunnels harboring the enemy and his supplies. It was McCarthy's hazardous job to squirm inside the burrows, which were too small to accommodate larger Americans, to somehow avoid the assorted scorpions, spiders, or giant Vietnamese rats, and flush out or kill any Viet Cong found there.

After twelve months of combat duty, he returned home in 1966 with his body punctured with shrapnel, a bronze star for valor, and eight other battlefield decorations. He was reassigned to duty as a drill sergeant at Fort Dix, N.J. McCarthy had planned a career in the Army and had served a tour of duty in the Republic of Korea prior to being sent to Vietnam. But he was disenchanted with the manner in which the United States was waging the war.

"There was just no way that I could rationalize preparing new guys at Fort Dix to go over to Vietnam and get shot up in a war this country didn't want to win," he recalls today. "The only thing to do was to get out." His Army career lasted almost exactly four years.

Even though his physical condition was deteriorating because of his wounds, McCarthy brought the same courage and bulldog tenacity he had shown as a point man with the Big Red One to his new undertaking as an advocate for Vietnam veterans—first with the Vietnam Veterans Unification and later with the AOVI. At first run from an office in McCarthy's Manhattan apartment, with support from Reutershan's mother and sister in Westchester, the AOVI was eventually expanded to about a dozen branch offices around the country, all staffed by veterans and members of their families.

Soon after the Ryans' first meeting with McCarthy, they were appearing and speaking at meetings with veterans and at press conferences, carrying their story about Agent Orange and the government's laissez-faire attitude concerning the plight of the Vietnam veterans to the media and to the public.

Their story was told in newspapers, magazines, over radio and television. Television film crews traveled from Germany, Japan, England, Ireland, Sweden, France and

Italy to Long Island to photograph and interview the Ryans. Michael accepted a position as a senior vice president of the AOVI, and Maureen became an honorary vice president. Their names appear on the masthead of the organization's newsletter, published whenever money is available, with those of other AOVI leaders, including the names of Reutershan and that of another deceased member, Edmund P. Juteau, Jr., a former combat medic who died of cancer in 1980, age thirty.

As Michael and Maureen expanded their activities, their home became a communications center for the campaign to alert veterans of the danger from exposure to the deadly chemicals sprayed so casually in Vietnam, and to force the Veterans Administration and other government agencies to provide health care and other benefits. Veterans and members of their families telephoned the Ryans from all over the country.

They received calls from frightened veterans who had heard their names and phoned to talk about their illnesses, about their shaky marriages, or their deformed babies. Some veterans were angry and emotional, threatening to take up rifles and put their combat training to use shooting government bureaucrats and chemical company executives. Calling upon his police training and street psychology, Michael reasoned with them until they became calm.

"There's been enough violence," he would advise. "We'll fight them, but we're not going to allow them to drag us down to their level."

Others were suicidal. They had to be soothed and convinced that it was important for them to be strong and to save themselves for the struggle with the powerful forces of the Pentagon, the VA, and the chemical companies. Statistics compiled by both the AOVI and the VA indicate that the Vietnam veterans have a suicide rate four times as high as the average of American veterans of earlier wars.

The Ryans told callers about the AOVI and other organizations, and often helped them to reach veterans living in their areas. Maureen talked to the wives and mothers about birth defects, about reduced sex drives among Agent Orange veterans, and about genetic counseling. If they lived within a reasonable driving distance, she would invite them to visit, and a few days later the coffeepot would be perking on the stove while the Ryans sat in their kitchen talking with guests about Agent Orange.

One couple brought their five-day-old daughter to the Ryan home after a doctor had arranged for them to meet. The father was a former Marine, and the mother was a nurse. Their little girl's hands were attached directly to her shoulders, like those of so many of the Thalidomide babies born twenty-five years earlier. One hand had only three, tiny, deformed pink fingers attached to it. The other was an almost exact twin of Kerry's.

The distress of the parents was touchingly apparent. They behaved as though they were in shock. Mike and Maureen knew the feeling. They had been there. They had also arranged for Michael's parents and his sister to visit.

It was a hot summer afternoon and the little house was packed with people. When the infant's mother began to remove the child's dress because of the gathering heat, Maureen and her mother-in-law descended on them. They swept the baby up and began cuddling her, marveling at her beauty. Maureen peered down at the baby and gasped: "My God, that's Kerry's hand."

She asked Kerry to pull up her sleeve so that the adults could make the comparison. The similarity was unmistakable.

Kerry and her family had survived physical and emotional trauma very similar to that of their guests. Yet when the visiting couple looked around them, everyone was smiling, laughing, joking, and having a good time. Kerry was very much a part of it all.

Sometime later when the couple left, they were smiling, too. The baby's mother was carrying copies of two books, *The Pendulum and the Toxic Cloud* and *The Poison That Fell from the Sky,** considered to be classics of reporting about the dangers of dioxin and chemical poisons in our society. The nurse was already convinced that Agent Orange was responsible for the imperfect birth of her baby. Her husband was unconvinced, although his Marine unit had been in a heavily sprayed area of Vietnam. Military authorities had assured their men the chemical spray was not dangerous to humans, and the ex-Marine was holding on to the fiction that there was another cause.

The gravel was crunching under the wheels of their car as the couple pulled out of the driveway when Vicky Ryan turned to Maureen and soberly advised: "You know, that little kid's got a heart defect?"

"Yes, I know," Maureen replied, thinking back to the hours she had spent watching over her daughter in intensive-care nurseries before Kerry's damaged heart was repaired. "I didn't like the way the baby was breathing when I was holding her." Maureen later telephoned the child's doctor and informed him of her suspicions. He assured her that she was wrong.

Two weeks later the baby was taken to the Rusk Institute at New York University Hospital for tests. Doctors

---

The Pendulum and the Toxic Cloud: The Course of Dioxin Contamination, by Thomas Whiteside, Yale University Press, New Haven, 1979; and *The Poison That Fell from the Sky,* by John G. Fuller, Random House, New York, 1977.

diagnosed a ventricular septical defect in her heart, the same defect Kerry was born with.

The doctor who made the primary diagnosis had previously treated Italian children with similar congenital abnormalities, and after completing the examination, she walked into the hallway to talk with the little girl's parents. "I don't know where you were," she told them, "but this baby's birth defects were chemically induced."

The baby's father simply nodded his head. There was nothing left to argue about. His daughter was a victim of Agent Orange.

By 1980 nearly 300 groups had been formed across the United States seeking to focus public attention on the continuing problems of Vietnam veterans. The size of the organizations varied from an estimated 10,000 members or more in the AOVI and other large groups such as the Vietnam Veterans of America and the Vetline-Hotline (headquartered in the Chicago area), to smaller regional groups like the Vietnam Veterans of South Dakota. Some are composed of no more than a few dozen members. Each has a story worth telling.

Ron DeYoung is a Vietnam-era veteran who never served in Southeast Asia. DeYoung matriculated directly into the U.S. Army Military Academy at West Point after graduating from high school in South Holland, Illinois, a southern suburb of Chicago. He was a cadet for about six weeks, when he realized he didn't want a career as an Army officer after all. He left the Academy and entered the inactive reserve while attending college for a year, then went on active duty as an enlisted man. After duty in Germany he returned to the United States to serve out his enlistment as a trumpeter with the Army band. While with the band, he played taps at the funerals of thirteen soldiers killed in Vietnam.

DeYoung was discharged in 1968, and ten years later was working at Columbia College when he met Maude DeVictor. Her thesis and the evidence she had accumulated to support it were compelling. Mrs. DeVictor had put together a ghastly record of case histories from veterans and their family members that indicated chemical sprays used in Vietnam were probably carcinogenic and teratogenic in man. DeYoung began talking with people who worked with veterans at other colleges in the Chicago area and helped establish an ad hoc consortium.

An organization named CAVEAT emerged from the consortium. CAVEAT concentrated much of its efforts on public relations, contacting the media, and spreading the story of Agent Orange. Seminars on Agent Orange were sponsored in the Midwest, literature was distributed, and officials dealing with veterans' affairs on state levels in the Midwest were informed and advised of the needs of veterans thought to have been exposed to toxic chemicals.

DeYoung and CAVEAT helped form the National Veterans Task Force on Agent Orange in 1978 at a convention of the National Association of Concerned Veterans in Kansas City, Missouri. Scientists, lawyers, and church organizations joined with veterans' groups as components of and supporters of the new coalition currently headquartered in St. Louis.

The first project called for assisting the American Health Foundation, headquartered in New York City, to conduct a nationwide epidemiological study of Vietnam veterans. DeYoung, who became temporary chairman before passing the gavel to John Furst in St. Louis, said questionnaires would be mailed to veterans in an effort to carry out the thorough study neglected by federal agencies. Unable to unite all Vietnam veterans' advocates into one monolithic organization, each group in the task force was assigned a specific target. CAVEAT's project is the VA and its approach to the problems of the Vietnam veteran, with special focus on victims of Agent Orange.

Chris Johnson organized the Vietnam Veterans of South Dakota from his home in Rapid City eleven years after he graduated from high school and volunteered for the draft. He was classified 1-A, and believed the recruiter who told him that if he volunteered, he would have a better choice of schools. The Army trained him as a machine gunner and assigned him to Mike Ryan's former outfit, the Eleventh Armored Cavalry, as a crew member on an APC.

The nineteen-year-old from the Black Hills didn't mind the assignment all that much and, in fact, deliberately arranged to be sent to Vietnam. His brother, Bill, served two years in the Army, and his father, Richard, spent three years in the Pacific during World War II. Schooled in the unquestioning patriotism of his middle-American background, Johnson looked forward to his service in the war zone as an opportunity to serve his country and become a man. By the time he was twenty, on January 17, 1970, he was in the thick of it.

Johnson's assault group was patrolling about a mile and a half from the Cambodian border one day when they uncovered a huge bunker complex in the jungle. The enemy had obviously faded back into the underbrush only minutes before, because cooked rice was left behind and it was still warm. There was no one left to fight, so the Americans left the area and camped for the night planning to return the next day.

Johnson was manning an M-60 machine gun on the lead

APC when his unit's armored vehicles and their crews pushed back into the jungle toward the bunker complex. They had barely penetrated the jungle when a rocket-propelled grenade slammed into the front of Johnson's vehicle disabling the driver. A moment later another grenade struck the cupulo where the sergeant in charge of the APC was manning a 50-caliber machine gun. He was blown off onto the ground.

Johnson grabbed his M-16 rifle and leaped down running to help the sergeant. Behind him, another grenade exploded against the crippled vehicle. The sergeant had been stunned but was not seriously injured and he waved Johnson away. Johnson sprinted for the next vehicle in line, turning and firing his M-16 as he ran, until he exhausted his ammunition.

His APC had stopped dead in its tracks, and as he looked behind him, he expected to see the rest of the crew following. Instead one of the crewman was waving his arm, motioning for Johnson to return. Johnson dashed back carrying his empty rifle and scrambled onto the vehicle. He took over one of the machine guns as the other gunner turned and dropped inside the APC to lift out the wounded driver. Johnson squeezed the trigger of the machine gun. It was empty. He bent over to grab ammunition to reload, and as he straightened up the next grenade exploded against the vehicle, hurling him across it. Dazed, he peered down at his right leg. A small piece of muscle about as big around as his finger was all that was attaching his lower leg to his knee. He crawled off the APC and began dragging himself along the ground toward the rear of the column, looking for a medic.

His damaged leg didn't hurt. The sensation was similar to that of a limb when the circulation is briefly cut off, causing it to tingle. The pain started when he began catching his leg on sharp bamboo stubs splintered a few

inches from the ground during the battle. Pain swept over
him then in dizzying shockwaves, and he had to stop, pull
his leg free, and continue crawling. He was still conscious
and looking for help when a medic finally reached him,
applied a tourniquet above the knee, and administered
other first aid. It was March 5, 1970, and Chris Johnson
had just earned a Bronze Star for Valor and a Purple
Heart in exchange for his right leg and shrapnel damage
to his left hip and right arm. Airlifted back to the U.S., he
was fitted with a prosthetic leg at an Army hospital. Fortu-
nately the damage was below the knee, and his precious
kneecap was saved.

After thirteen months of hospitalization he returned
home, where he soon met a local girl, married her, and
began putting weight on his slender 130-pound, five-foot,
ten-inch body. His wife, Colleen, is a good cook, and Johnson rapidly ballooned to 175 pounds. It was 1976, and a
good year for Johnson and his wife. They had their first
child, Nathan, a healthy boy. Then the trouble started.
Johnson began to experience dizzy spells, he had frequent
chills, and his weight began to drop. The symptoms were
similar to influenza, and the ailment persisted until his
weight was reduced again to 130 pounds.

An acnelike rash he was first bothered with in the hospital continued to plague him. Ugly pimplelike sores
popped out in nasty blackhead-centered bumps behind
his ears and on his shoulders, and sometimes spread to his
jaw and lips. They made him feel dirty. He went to the VA
hospital and had some of them lanced, but they returned
worse than ever before. A dermatologist at the hospital
advised him that he had "sebaceous activity of the
glands," a condition commonly observed in people with
oily skin.

Previously a moderate drinker, Johnson had completely
cut off his intake of alcohol. Even a small amount caused

him to have trouble with his balance, and led to unpleasant stomach upsets and severe headaches. His stomach was often tender, and he had to be extremely cautious about what he ate because the wrong foods at the wrong time were followed by severe chest pains or other allergic reactions. His vision began to bother him, and he had special trouble with depth perception. Some of his difficulty, doctors said, was caused by irritable bowel syndrome, spastic colon.

Colleen became pregnant with their second child. During a Christmas vacation trip to Georgia, she began experiencing so much pain he took her to an Army hospital near Atlanta for treatment. Doctors said her body was behaving almost as if it were trying to abort. But she carried the baby full term, and on August 25, after almost twenty-four hours of labor, she delivered a second son. His intestines and liver were attached to the outside of his body, and the passages in his nose and mouth were so abnormally thin the doctors couldn't attach aspirators. Struggling to breathe, he was flown to a hospital in Denver that had more sophisticated life-support equipment for infants. He died within five hours after his birth.

The Johnsons were told that their son had had twenty-six congenital abnormalities. He had cysts on his brain, a flattened head, a hole in his heart, deformed arms and legs, club feet, and stiff fingers that overlapped. His ears were lower than normal on the sides of his head, and the roof of his mouth was deformed. An autopsy disclosed that he also had chromosomal abnormalities.

Neither of the baby's parents had family histories of congenital defects, and they assumed the abnormal development of the fetus was an accident. They believed it was merely chance that had selected them as parents of a malformed infant. They wanted another child, so they had their chromosomes tested. They were normal, so another baby was conceived. As the fetus developed, doctors monitored its progress with amnioscentesis. It appeared to be developing normally, and in February 1980, a girl, Nicolle, was born. She was slightly smaller than the average infant, but was otherwise normal and apparently healthy.

Colleen was pregnant with Nicolle when Johnson first read about Agent Orange in a copy of *DAV,* the official magazine of the Disabled American Veterans. He observed another article about the suspicious chemical spray program at about the same time in *The Rapid City Journal.* The stories described Vietnam veterans who had returned home and, while still in their twenties or early thirties, had become victims of strange and difficult-to-diagnose illnesses.

A veteran from South Dakota whom Johnson had met shortly after being evacuated from Vietnam was quoted describing the symptoms. The ex-GI, Roger Andal, had become an aide to South Dakota Congressman Tom Daschle after discharge from the service. Andal told of men who complained of shortness of breath, false heart attacks, decreased sex drive, mysterious mood changes, and chloracne. He also told of their wives who suffered miscarriages and stillbirths, or gave birth to babies with multiple congenital abnormalities.

Johnson's thoughts returned to his early weeks in Vietnam when he rode APCs that rumbled through jungles with grotesquely misshapen trees that were as barren as telephone poles. There was a complete absence of animal noises in the strangely dead areas. But the young soldier didn't worry about it at the time. He assumed the trees were merely very old. And small animals may have been frightened away by the noise of the heavy armored vehicles, accounting for the quiet. Johnson's home was about twenty-five miles from Mount Rushmore in the middle of the Black Hills, and he had never seen a jungle before. So he accepted the silent Vietnamese wasteland as it was.

It was ten years before he finally learned why the jungle was so silent and dead. He began to wonder then too about the respiratory problems he once experienced in Vietnam. His chest suddenly tightened up one day and it became so difficult and painful for him to breathe he couldn't walk. He was sent to an aid station in Bien-Hoa, where he described the pleurisylike attack to a medic. The medic peered at his tongue, tapped his chest a couple of times, and fed him two aspirin tablets. The examination was over, and the medic advised him to walk to the rear of the tent and lie down for a while on one of the cots. "You'll probably get over it," he advised. The medic was apparently correct. The next day Johnson was back on duty.

The similarities between the symptoms described in the stories about Agent Orange, and Johnson's troubles were disturbingly similar. But the suspicions tapping at his consciousness weren't the kind he wanted to accept. He attempted to convince himself that his illnesses were nothing more than the result of delayed stress due to the danger of combat in Vietnam and the trauma of his injuries. The birth of his second son was just one of those things that sometimes happens to people, he told himself.

Yet, the similarities between his medical problems and the imperfect birth of the baby nagged at him. He contacted Andal. Andal advised Congressman Daschle that he was in touch with a veteran in their district who was a possible victim of the chemical spray program in Vietnam.

Johnson continued to gather information about Agent Orange, and he was finally convinced that he had returned home with traces of dioxin in his body. He and his wife agreed there would be no more children.

Johnson began assisting the Congressman, working to inform other veterans and the public about the toxic nightmare being experienced by American servicemen and their allies in Vietnam.

He testified in Washington before the Subcommittee on Medical Facilities and Benefits of the Congressional Committee on Veterans Affairs. Johnson returned home from the hearings and founded the Vietnam Veterans of South Dakota, demanding that the government provide proper health care and other benefits for victims of Agent Orange. He was attracting attention and the kind of publicity that the VA would rather avoid, and a few days after his return home, he was reached by the agency and asked if he had filed a disability claim based on his symptoms of dioxin poisoning. He had.

For some reason he says he hasn't been able to clearly ascertain, a transcription of his Congressional testimony was entered in his medical records at the Fort Meade VA Hospital near Rapid City. The VA notified him shortly after that his one hundred percent unemployability benefits were being reduced to sixty percent. When he questioned the action, he was told that it was because he had been retrained and was rehabilitated. He had attended electronics school for a time on the GI Bill but had to quit; he was too sick to continue attending classes.

Consequently he stays home a lot and has had time to take calls from agitated veterans who have finally learned why they've been sick most of the time since returning from Vietnam, why they've frightened or chased away their wives with violent outbursts of temper, and why their babies were born dead or with terrible abnormalities.

Johnson and his organization, which he operates from

his home, work closely with other Vietnam veteran advocate groups, including the AOVI, the Vietnam Veterans of America—and the Veterans Leadership Conference.

Headquartered in Chicago, the VLC is headed by a woman. Intense and articulate, Joan Maiman is a Navy admiral's daughter who spent a year in Vietnam during 1970 and 1971 with the Red Cross. She is one of thousands of American women, military and civilian, who served in Vietnam during the hostilities.

Records dealing with American civilians in Vietnam are inadequate or missing altogether, but thousands served, including representatives of the USO, church groups, the Merchant Marines and private business, as well as the Red Cross. Apparently no individual or agency has cumulative data on exact numbers of American civilians who were in Vietnam or who may have been exposed to Agent Orange and its sister herbicides there. But enough is known today so that Joan Maiman knows she is among more than 2.4 million Americans who may now be, or who may become in the future, victims of dioxin poisoning as a result of exposure to herbicides and insecticides used in Vietnam.

Now a slight 122 pounds and five-foot, four-inches, the VLC chief cheerfully admits that she was several pounds heavier and "a chubby little kid" of twenty-two when she graduated from Trinity College in Washington, D.C., with a degree in sociology and volunteered for duty with the Red Cross in Vietnam. She was sent to the Army's 24th Evacuation Hospital at Long Binh to counsel wounded soldiers.

She spoke fluent French and was sometimes utilized as an interpreter, leading her to travel far more extensively in the former French colony than most American women in Vietnam. She accompanied medical teams to outlying Vietnamese villages to assist in treatment of civilians. At the request of the government of South Vietnam for a time, she also used her knowledge of French to teach English to a group of Vietnamese nuns near Long Binh. But after being bombarded with mortar fire three times by Viet Cong in the supposedly pacified area, she abandoned the effort.

Once when she was hurrying to lift a patient out of a bed during a rocket attack on the evacuation hospital, she strained her back, severely enough so that she herself became a bed patient. She began losing weight while she was hospitalized, and by the time she returned to the United States to work at the Veterans Hospital at Valley Forge, Pennsylvania, she had lost twenty pounds.

She was also experiencing other health problems she hadn't had before. She broke out in rashes eight times, with unsightly sores that doctors consistently diagnosed as German measles—a disease that can be contracted only once. One doctor finally decided that the ailment was impetigo.

Her immune system appeared to be shattered. She couldn't stand changes in temperature. Warm weather left her feverish, and cool temperatures left her freezing cold. She couldn't tolerate alcohol. Even a few sips of an alcoholic beverage brought on splitting headaches, causing her to break out in a rash and to have difficulty breathing. Rubbing alcohol made her sneeze if she so much as smelled it. Direct exposure to the sun caused her skin to blister, and the pigmentation changed, spotting her flesh with ugly mottles of purple and white.

Joan began reading magazine and newspaper stories about Agent Orange. It wasn't difficult to make the connection between her service in Vietnam with the Red Cross and the sudden negative change in her health. What she suspected, and later verified to her own satisfaction, frightened and angered her.

She decided to do something about it and organized a

picnic and day of unification attended by forty-five Chicago area veterans' groups in Chicago's Grant Park on Memorial Day, 1979. Among more than 5,000 men and women who mingled at the unique event were members of such diverse groups as the American Legion, VFW, Amvets, Afro-American Vets, Black Veterans Association, CAVEAT, Gold Star Wives and Mothers, Vietnam Veterans Against the War, and a contingent of Montford Point Marines.

Joined later by John Monaghan, a former Air Force cargo handler at Cam Ranh Bay, and members of twenty organizations represented at the Day in the Park, she applied to the White House Federal Veterans Coordinating Committee and to the VA for funding for a community-based organization to serve as an advocate for the estimated 250,000 Vietnam veterans in the Greater Chicago area.

Angered at the lack of a response after waiting eleven months, the group finally put together its own action program to work for veterans in the primary areas of medical needs, mental health, social services, economics, and legislation. The Chicago Leadership Conference was officially born. It was May 15, 1980.

The coalition launched special efforts to reach Black and Hispanic veterans, who it was believed were less likely to be informed of the Agent Orange controversy, and has coordinated various activities with civil rights organizations such as Operation PUSH, the National Association for the Advancement of Colored People, and the Urban League.

By 1980 the CLC had become the Veterans Leadership Conference, and was national in scope, functioning as an umbrella organization for many other veterans rights advocacy groups. The VLC had even begun to attract interest and participation from such traditional veterans organizations as the American Legion and Veterans of Foreign Wars.

In contrast, the VA and other government agencies have done nothing, or very little, to make the job easier. Anyone who has contended for very long with the government over the Agent Orange issue has learned quickly that agencies such as the VA, the DOD, and the Air Force are willing to act only when they were pushed. Still, a handful of sympathetic national legislators has helped. First among them was the late Senator Philip Hart of Michigan, who conducted a seminal legislative hearing on Agent Orange. Others prominently connected to the introduction or support of legislation to help veterans exposed to Agent Orange include the already mentioned Congressman Tom Daschle, the late Congressman Ralph Metcalf of Illinois, Congressman David Bonior of Michigan, and Senators Alan Cranston of California and Charles H. Percy of Illinois.

The Ryans testified before House and Senate committees investigating veterans' claims of health problems related to exposure to toxic chemicals in Vietnam, of denials by the VA of responsibility for subsequent health care, and denials of culpability by the DOD and various chemical companies. John and Mildred Woods of Hempstead, N.Y., testified with the Ryans on June 26, 1979, at the first session of a hearing by the Congressional Subcommittee on Oversight and Investigation of the Interstate and Foreign Commerce Committee in Washington, D.C.

Eight-year-old Kerry, bright and alert, with her straight, brown hair cut short, was dressed in a crisp sunsuit for the hearings. She sat between her parents and Bobby Muller as she watched the drama unfold. Like Kerry, Muller was in a wheelchair.

Michael and Maureen talked of their daughter's birth, of the multiple malformations that so nearly cost her life, and of Michael's health problems that are so symptomatic of dioxin poisoning. Michael complained to the committee that veterans had been used as human guinea pigs. He assured the lawmakers, nevertheless, that he loved his country and would serve again if called. "But I want this country to get back the way it was," he said. "I want the veterans treated right. I want treatment for my daughter."

Although he insisted that it is the duty of VA hospitals to make treatment available to children whose health and physical well-being have been damaged by dioxin carried home in the bodies of their fathers from Vietnam, he stressed he would never permit Kerry to be treated in one of the facilities.

"That," he said, "would be like giving me a gift certificate to an empty store."

Maureen told the legislators she had initially accepted Kerry's birth as "something God gave me." But after learning that the chemicals sprayed in Vietnam were responsible, she said, she was bitter. "Now I realize Kerry had every right to be on a bicycle instead of in a wheelchair. I have an eight-year-old child who is still in Pampers."

Woods also told the Congressmen of his ill health, and of the sons born after his return from Vietnam, where he pushed through the dust-choked and wilting jungles near Long Binh. He traced his exposure to late summer after his unit had secured an area and watched almost daily as aircraft sprayed jungle near a hill nicknamed "Suicide Mountain." The chemical sometimes drifted into his compound, he told the panel. "Within two to ten weeks, I started losing weight. I went from two hundred pounds down to a hundred thirty-nine pounds."

When he reported to VA hospitals with complaints of stomach cramps, chest pains, false heart attacks, temporary blindness, or headaches, Woods said, tests inexplicably indicated there was nothing wrong with him, and the VA refused to pay his medical bills. His veterans' disability pension was dropped from thirty percent to twenty percent, then to ten percent, then to nothing. "The doctors think I'm crazy," he asserted.

"When I hit those battlefields in Vietnam, my sons were with me." Woods told the panel. "My sons are the real veterans. And Mike Ryan's daughter was with him. She's a veteran. Help them."

Government representatives spoke of the difficulty of documentation. Subsequently a bill to aid Agent Orange victims was defeated. The VA spoke of a six-year Air Force study to be completed in 1985! Despite growing criticism of their policies and inaction—often from official government sources—the VA, the DOD, and major chemical companies refused to take responsibility or to offer assistance. It seemed that the only recourse of the Agent Orange victims would be found in the courtroom.

9

A MATTER
OF LAW

On March 19, 1979, the Ryans and nineteen other couples
were listed as plaintiffs in an unprecedented class-action
product-liability suit filed by Victor Yannacone against
the Dow Chemical Company and five other manufacturers of defoliants and herbicides sprayed in Vietnam.

The unique federal action filed in the Long Island
branch of the U.S. Eastern District Court in Westbury,
N.Y., asked that all 2.8 million veterans who served in
Vietnam, along with their wives and children, be certified
as a class of plaintiffs. The plaintiffs sought:

—Immediate cessation of all advertising, promotion,
distribution, marketing, and sale of the contaminated herbicides.

—A declaration that the corporate defendants are trus-
tees of the public health, safety, and welfare, with a fiduci-
ary responsibility to protect the environment and its in-
habitants.

—Disclosure of all information in possession of the companies relating to the danger of the contaminated herbicides.

—Establishment by the companies of a tax-exempt court-administered reserve fund—initially estimated to be at least $4 billion—sufficient to cover damages resulting from use of the herbicide. The final point includes a stipulation providing for the reimbursement of the VA and Social Security Administration for benefits to compensate victims and their families and for use of funds to finance research into methods of treating victims of dioxin poisoning. Since the total potential liability exceeds the combined assets of the corporations, creation of the tax-exempt fund would provide a means of compensating the victims while permitting the continuation of business.

The class action was an outgrowth of a $10 million product liability suit filed in 1978 by an Islip, N.Y., law firm for Paul Reutershan against Dow. Reutershan's suit failed, but at his request, after his death McCarthy found a new legal champion in Yannacone. Yannacone expanded Reutershan's old petition and refiled it in the federal district court as a class action on behalf of individual veterans and family members associated with the AOVI.

"The Dow Chemical Company and a number of its competitors in the chemical industry conducted an enormous experiment on the health of American veterans who served in Vietnam and were exposed to phenoxy herbicides contaminated with dioxin which the companies knew could cause cancer, genetic damage, and birth defects," Yannacone said after filing.

The suit accused the companies of selling the herbicides "in wanton and reckless disregard for the public health, safety, and welfare." Eighteen classes of injury are spelled out, ranging from veterans with chloracne, veterans with cancer, the birth of malformed children, loss of sons and husbands, and individuals who might suffer damages in the future.

Named as defendants with Dow were the Diamond Shamrock Corporation of Cleveland; Hercules, Incorporated, of Wilmington, Delaware; the Monsanto Company of St. Louis; the Northwest Industries, Incorporated; and the North American Philips Corporation of Kansas City, Missouri. A few months later Northwest Industries and North American Philips Corporation were dropped from the case, and added on were Hoffman Taff Incorporated, Diamond Shamrock Company and Thompson-Hayward. Added in the spring of 1980 were the Hooker Chemical Company, a subsidiary of the Occidental Petroleum Corporation; and the Uniroyal Merchandising Company, a division of Uniroyal, Incorporated. Most of the companies are listed in the *Fortune 500*—a listing of the 500 largest and most powerful corporations in the United States. Yannacone cited a plethora of legal grounds for finding the chemical companies liable for damages. Among the grounds were breach of implied and expressed warranties to produce safe products, failure to adequately test products and warn of hazards, and failure to remove the potentially dangerous products from interstate commerce.

"We are dealing with a substance more toxic than anything that is regulated, more toxic than ionized radiation, plutonium, or radionuclides," Yannacone said.

A month after Yannacone filed the suit in Westbury, three law firms filed similar class actions in Chicago. Other suits were rapidly filed in cities and states throughout the nation. That summer, in a ruling that was an important victory for the veterans, presiding Judge George C. Pratt officially classified the suits as class actions, and they were consolidated under multilitigation status in Westbury, where the initial suits were filed. Judge Pratt observed that the case was unprecedented and that any decision he announced would, in effect, fashion "new law."

The massive suit and various actions and counter actions filed by attorneys for both the plaintiffs and the defense are producing intriguing and unique new legal concepts and problems.

Led by Dow, the chemical companies predictably responded to the assault with a spirited attack of their own. Among an avalanche of motions by company attorneys was a move for a court order enjoining Yannacone from discussing the case with outsiders. That in itself was not unique, but an aspect of the proposal that sought to prevent communication between counsel and veterans' organizations was unprecedented. The Vietnam Veterans Association filed to intervene, and through its attorneys argued against the motion, contending that the gag order violated the First Amendment and would contravene the right of veterans' organizations to obtain information about the litigation.

A victory for the veterans could create a host of problems. A massive monetary award in the billions of dollars would be crippling to even an industry as powerful as the chemical companies. It could also establish an historic and unpleasant—for the companies—legal precedent in the field of product liability. Hundreds of new chemical products are marketed every year, and a precedent setting judgment against the manufacturers would presumably leave the companies open for showers of future litigation.

Attorneys estimated that as many as 40,000 veterans may eventually become ill or die from effects of the toxicological cocktail unleashed on Vietnam. At least 2,000 children may be born with catastrophic deformities due to the chemical poisons their fathers carried home from the war.

The corporations marshaled a battalion of legal mercenaries against a broad array of legal talent assembled by the veterans as packages of new suits were filed around the country. Some of Wall Street's most high-priced law firms are among those hired by the war contractors.

In August 1979 Judge Pratt denied the motion for a gag order on the veterans' counsel, citing the First Amendment rights of organizations concerned with the Agent Orange issue to be informed. He also rejected the petition in the suit to ban manufacturing, advertising, distribution, and use of phenoxy herbicides in this country. In a nineteen-page decision, he explained that "primary jurisdiction" over herbicides belongs with the EPA. The matter should not be considered by the courts before it has been dealt with by the federal agency, he said.

As soon as they agreed to join in the suit, Michael and Maureen began driving south across Long Island to Yannacone's one-man office in Patchogue to help with typing, filing, proofreading, duplicating and stapling copies of briefs, motions, and other legal documents, and handling other clerical work necessary to continue the complex proceedings. For eight months they made the almost daily round-trip drive between Stony Brook and Patchogue, consistently accumulating 100-hour weeks. The gasoline bills began rivaling, then exceeding, their telephone bills. Yannacone eventually assembled three computerized data bases to compile information. The Ryans were also dispatched to Chicago, Los Angeles, and other major cities where groups of veterans were joining the class action, to meet with lawyers, ex-GIs and members of their families. Yannacone and other lawyers for the veterans defrayed the expenses of transportation, hotels, and other costs.

Working so closely with Yannacone, the Ryans developed a close relationship with the peripatetic environmental attorney, as well as a healthy respect for his facile mind and dogged determination. Yannacone had followed his father, a personal injury and workmen's compensation lawyer, into the legal profession. But before he took up law, he studied chemistry, physics, mathematics, and zoology for three years at Syracuse University and at Kalamazoo College prior to enrolling in Brooklyn Law School. He did graduate work at the New York Law School after passing his bar examination. His exposure to such a variety of different subjects during his early college years equipped him with an invaluable and utilitarian background for his trail-blazing legal specialty in environmental law.

Law and the environment are emotional issues for Yannacone, and are capable, singularly or in concert, of evoking his intense outrage when he suspects that either is being abused.

While molding a reputation as the nation's foremost environmental lawyer, the eclectic attorney has somehow made time to excel as a father and husband, obtain a commercial radio-telephone license, play the baritone saxophone, and perform as a member of the Brookhaven Symphony Orchestra. But it is for his expertise in environmental law and for his precedent-establishing assaults on the giant corporations and governmental bodies that would pollute and destroy our precious land, water, and air that he is best known.

The flamboyant and hard-driving lawyer has ranged far and wide in his crusade against the polluters. His campaign has led to the preservation of the Florissant fossil beds in Colorado; action against the U.S. Army Corps of Engineers that succeeded in halting construction of the Cross Florida Barge Canal after partial completion of the ecologically devastating project; and litigation which led to a temporary injunction order by the New York State Supreme Court against use of DDT, Dieldrin, and other broad-spectrum, nonpersistent pesticides by the Suffolk County Mosquito Control Commission. He filed the action against DDT on behalf of his wife, Carol A. Yannacone, who, as plaintiff, sued individually and on behalf of all the people of Suffolk County. It marked the first time a suit not involving a personal damage claim was ever brought against environmental degradation.

Although Judge Jack Stanislaw ruled that the legislature, rather than the court, had final responsibility for determining if the use of DDT should be regulated or eliminated, the commission switched to use of less persistent chemicals during the period of the injunction.

Yannacone is coauthor with Bernard S. Cohen and Steven G. Davison of the two-volume legal treatise *Environmental Rights and Remedies* and has produced nearly 100 papers and articles on environmental and real-estate law. His national reputation, however, is more closely tied to his seminal role in litigation that contributed to the permanent prohibition in this country of DDT, probably the best known and, at one time, the most popular pesticide in the world.

In 1969 Yannacone and other elements of the Environmental Defense Fund carried the struggle against DDT to Wisconsin in what developed into a six-month open forum before the State Department of Natural Resources. The environmentalists attracted national attention in a successful effort to have DDT declared a pollutant according to the state's water quality provisions. The bitterly contested hearing pitted Yannacone and the EDF-led environmentalists against a glittering array of chemical industry lawyers, scientists, and executives banded together as the National Agricultural Chemicals Association's Indus-

try Task Force for DDT. A transcript of the prolonged
hearing weighed forty pounds and numbered 4,499
pages.

The confrontation ended in such an obvious victory for
the environmental and conservationist forces that they
promptly filed suits against the U.S. Department of Agriculture, demanding a nationwide ban on DDT. Yannacone personally filed a $30 billion class action in federal
court on behalf of his wife and all present and future
Americans, against eight manufacturers of DDT. The suit
asks recovery of damages, and charges the manufacturers
with false advertising and conspiracy to withhold information from the American people about the long-term
harmful effects of DDT on the environment.

During Yannacone's battle against DDT, he defined the
basic concepts of environmental law, citing the right of
Americans "of this generation and of those generations
yet unborn" to a clean and healthful environment. His
arguments were based upon the Fifth, Ninth, and Four-
teenth Amendments of the U.S. Constitution.

Prior to publication of Rachel Carson's *Silent Spring*
and of legal and legislative assaults on the dangerous in-
secticide by Yannacone and other perceptive environmentalists and conservationists, DDT was widely ac-
claimed for relieving worldwide food shortages and
reducing malaria.

The hearings in Wisconsin ultimately led to loss by the
U.S. Department of Agriculture of direct responsibility
for the regulation of pesticides, and in 1972 the EPA can-
celed all except public health and quarantine uses of
DDT. The wonder pesticide was belatedly recognized as
being dispersed rather than diluted when it was released
into the environment, permitting it to enter the food
chain to accumulate in higher animal forms and dangerously affect animal reproduction. Some scientists believe,

but have not been able to prove, that human reproduction may be damaged by accumulation of DDT in the body as well.

The homily that lawsuits should only be resorted to if every other legal means to settle disputes has failed has no place in Yannacone's philosophy. He feels that litigation is like a club: If it isn't wielded, it becomes a dead weight. All major social changes that have enriched American life share a genesis in fundamental constitutional litigation, he believes. It is necessary to file suits to prompt legislative action.

Conservationists especially find it difficult to attract either the attention or concern of legislators, and litigation, that "short of bloody revolution," is the most effective means of forcibly focusing their concern on environmental interests, according to the attorney.

A crucial element of the complex suit against the manufacturers of Agent Orange was upheld on November 20, 1979, when Judge Pratt ruled that the litigation would be handled under federal common law rather than federal diversity. The judge wrote that his opinion was based on the fact that "the estimated number of involved veterans ranges from thousands to millions, and the estimated potential liability of the . . . war contractors ranges from millions to billions of dollars. Application of varying state laws would burden federal interests by creating uncertainty as to the rights of both veterans and war contractors." On the same day the judge rejected an argument by the companies contending that the claims should be handled solely by the VA.

But the second U.S. Circuit Court of Appeals in New York ruled two-to-one against the veterans when Judge Pratt's decision permitting prosecution of the suit under federal common law was appealed. In December 1981 the U.S. Supreme Court voted seven-to-two to uphold the

Appeals court decision. Only Justices Harry A. Blackmun and Sandra Day O' Connor voted to hear the appeal on behalf of an estimated two million veterans and members of their families.

There are broad differences in state statutes governing limitations of time during which an injured party may sue for damages; thus, the decision to consider the suit under federal common law was of critical importance to the veterans. Some states have statutes of limitations which provide no more than three years during which aggrieved persons may file liability suits after discovery of injury. Others are less restrictive and allow a decade or more for filing. Thus a veteran from Illinois would be able to file for damages ten years after discovery of injury, while a veteran in New York had only three years from point of injury to file.

The Supreme Court denial had its greatest impact on more than 600,000 veterans now living in Alabama, Alaska, Arkansas, Colorado, Georgia, Idaho, Maine, Mississippi, Montana, Nebraska, New York, Nevada, North Carolina, North Dakota, Rhode Island, South Dakota, Utah, Virginia, West Virginia and Wisconsin.

Michael Ryan and other veterans were chagrined at the decision, which they consider unfair. "I wasn't sent to Vietnam as a resident of New York. I went as an American, and we deserve to have the case tried together as Americans, not as New Yorkers, Californians, or Texans," he complained.

A few months after Yannacone filed the massive class action in Westbury, a team of attorneys associated with the New York-based Citizen Soldier organization filed suits on behalf of more than 100 individual veterans and their survivors or families in a Federal District Court in Texas. Eschewing a class action, they based their litigation on third-party products liability, contending that the basic conflict existed between the government and the chemical companies. They indicated that they believed individual lawsuits would promote larger settlements than a class action.

Frank McCarthy said that some other lawyers motivated more by greed than by any sincere desire to help veterans contacted him and offered "fifty dollars a head" for every Agent Orange victim he could refer to them as a client, he said. One attorney advised McCarthy that he could accumulate a large amount of money by charging veterans four hundred dollars each to file and process claims. McCarthy said there were also some organizations "trying to use the veterans' misery to make money."

Yannacone conceded that he had also been approached by wealthy lawyers and other potential backers with offers to finance the suit if he would agree to settle for millions instead of continuing to insist on billions of dollars, and consequently risking years of additional litigation. Agreement to the proposal would mean that many veterans would be left out of the settlement, which he considers to be unconscionable, the attorney said. Yannacone and other consortium attorneys financed the class action out of their own pockets, under a contingency arrangement providing for repayment of expenses. Fees were to be determined by a judge at the conclusion of litigation.

Bolstered by national publicity and the dissemination of information by veterans' groups, the suit burgeoned. Within two years the number of individual plaintiffs had swollen to more than 7,000, and Yannacone was chief counsel for a consortium of some 1,250 lawyers from 150 law firms. The suit was the largest such action ever filed in an American court, and attorneys for the veterans described it as being "as federal as the U.S. Constitution."

Forty Vietnam veterans from Australia, organized as

the Viet-Nam [sic] Veterans Action Association, also joined in the suit, sending attorney William McMillan to New York to file on behalf of themselves and their children. McCarthy observed that the Australians have experienced "the same stigma and poor treatment" as American veterans and have had difficulty obtaining proper attention and care from their government for their Agent Orange related problems.

In January 1980 separate surprise motions seeking to designate the U.S. government as a third party in the suit were filed by each of the defendant chemical companies. The companies asserted that if the veterans were harmed by Agent Orange as alleged, that it was the fault of the government, not of the manufacturers. Although the suits varied somewhat in detail, they charged basically the following:

—The government failed to conduct adequate testing of Agent Orange before it was used.

—The government did not use Agent Orange properly, applied it indiscriminately, in high concentrations, and failed to properly instruct and protect the servicemen who handled it.

—Both the DOD and the VA compounded the problems by neglecting to warn veterans of the health consequence of exposure and to provide treatment. By failure to achieve early identification and treatment of the ailments, the impact of Agent Orange exposure was aggravated.

If the claims of the veterans were upheld, the suit asserted, the government should reimburse the companies. The company also asserted in a motion for dismissal that the chemicals were produced according to government specifications and the manufacturer had no control over the method of its use. They claimed that it was used in higher concentrations than they had recommended, adding that the government prevented them from attaching handling instructions or warning labels to the drums in which Agent Orange was shipped.

Dow Chemical Company spokesman Don Frayer was quoted in an article by writer Adrian Peracchio in Long Island's *Newsday* (March 17, 1980) as saying that the chemical manufacturers attempted unsuccessfully to convince the government to use Toridon, a safer herbicide, which was as effective as Agent Orange but less toxic and did not contain dioxin.

According to Peracchio, Yannacone responded to Dow's suit against the government by comparing it with the defense used at the Nuremberg War Crimes Trials by German arms manufacturers who supplied Hitler's war machine, in a bid to avoid paying reparations. That defense did not work at Nuremberg, and the veterans expected it to work no better in the U.S. Federal Courts, Yannacone declared. His prediction was correct. Judge Pratt dismissed the suit, ruling that the government is immune from prosecution in such cases.

In October 1980 Dow filed court documents indicating that the Army possessed knowledge of the potential danger of the contaminant dioxin in Agent Orange at least two years before the chemical was first used in Vietnam. The company cited a scientific paper published in 1962 in the *Journal of Investigative Dermatology* detailing tests for determining the dangers of dioxin by analyzing tissue from the ear of a live rabbit. The paper was based on a study financed by the Research and Development Division, Office of the Surgeon General, Department of the Army.

The paper also referred to another study of the toxicity of dioxin which was reported in a German scientific journal in 1957. In the document filed by Dow, the manufacturer contended that the federal government knew in

1962 that dioxin was an unavoidable by-product of the manufacturing process of 2,4,5-T, that dioxin was toxic, that it could be detected, and that it had been proved capable of causing liver damage, debilitation, loss of appetite, and chloracne in animals.

Dow charged in its brief that the government acted "negligently and recklessly" while violating the constitutional rights of its servicemen. Despite the accusations against the government, the war contractor continued to maintain, however incongruously, that Agent Orange was not hazardous to human health.

Predictably for a case contested by more than 1,000 lawyers and dealing with billions of dollars, the motions for discovery, subpoenaes, hearings, and other delays dragged on interminably. At a press conference, Yannacone predicted that the management techniques developed during litigation would become models for other major suits, such as anticipated action involving toxic waste dumps, tampon-related toxic-shock syndrome, and asbestos contamination. New legal moves were also frequently tested as the suit progressed slowly through the court.

In 1980 Judge Pratt ruled that a dying Vietnam veteran from the Philadelphia area could videotape his testimony, because he was not expected to live long enough to testify in person at the trial. Charlie Hartz was the only survivor of three veterans from southeastern Pennsylvania who joined in filing a brief included in the megasuit. Hartz, thirty-three, was dying of brain cancer, an ailment that had already claimed the lives of his two coplaintiffs. His attorneys argued that a videotape would better serve jurors considering his testimony than would a typed document. Judge Pratt agreed to videotaping of the statement, complete with aggressive cross-examination at the federal building in Philadelphia.

One of the major roadblocks faced by the veterans' legal consortium was refusal by the government to provide Air Force records of purchase and use of herbicides to aid in determining what chemicals were sprayed, where and when they were sprayed, and with what concentration of contaminants. Yannacone theorized that the government's attitude may mean that it has a hold-harmless agreement with the manufacturers. This would make taxpayers responsible for any damage from military use of the herbicides. The government was involved in an agreement of that type with manufacturers of pharmaceuticals during the swine flu controversy.

The uncooperative attitude of the government not only hindered prosecution of the suit, but also confronted many veterans with no-win situations in their dealings with the VA. "When this all started, these guys were told by the VA to provide verification of exposure," Chris Johnson explained. "And they were prevented from doing that because they needed Air Force documents that the government has refused in court to provide."

Although the VA eventually bowed to pressure to relax its demand that veterans provide proof of exposure before they could file Agent Orange injury claims, Johnson and several other members of the Vietnam Veterans of South Dakota decided to personally unearth the information necessary to correlate spraying missions with troop placement. The job was especially important to the South Dakota veterans. Seventy-eight percent of South Dakota's Vietnam era veterans were in combat, the highest percentage from any state in the nation.

Toiling for months, Johnson and his colleagues assembled more than 250 large-scale ground maps showing the terrain of South Vietnam, dates, and locations of ground troops. It was a slow, laborious job, which could not be undertaken until he obtained information pinpointing dates and locations of spray missions which were stored on computer tapes and printed in a book about three inches thick. Every spray mission by the Air Force was recorded there.

Scaled at one and one-half inches to the mile, the maps show the location of villages, military bases, and individual barracks and other buildings. Johnson matched the daily log of his unit activities with the maps and other information to trace the relationship of his personal whereabouts to spray areas, and made the maps available to other veterans so that they could do the same. It was a job that could have been accomplished by the DOD or other government agencies if they had cared to do it. And it is a job necessary to veterans, despite the relaxed VA requirement dealing with proof of exposure, because without knowledge of their personal susceptibility, they are missing a valuable tool necessary for accurate diagnosis of various mystery illnesses and are left unsure of their ability to father healthy, whole children.

As the South Dakota veterans were piecing together their maps and information in Rapid City, John Hansen, a Government Accounting Office employee in Washington was pulling together an inter-agency committee including representatives of the DOD, the VA, and other government departments, to uncover and organize information from Army records to help in the comparison of spray missions and Army troop locations. The job was made especially difficult because Army records had been unceremoniously dumped into boxes and hastily shoved into transport planes during the panicky American retreat from Saigon when South Vietnam fell to the Communists. Some 40,000 linear feet of records were collected and needed sorting, according to Hansen.

The increasingly intricate web of legal maneuvering became even more complicated with the filing of various corollary suits, including a class action by Yannacone against the VA. Top executives of the federal agency were named as codefendants in the action, which charged the VA with permitting unlicensed doctors to practice medicine on Vietnam veterans, issuing of psychotropic drugs, burying Agent Orange claims, violating the constitutional rights of veterans, and other offenses. Veterans across the country joined in the suit, filing briefs and charging specific VA hospitals with gross and negligent malpractice.

There were certain similarities between the VA suit filed by Yannacone and another class-action suit against the agency filed by an organization called Vetline-Hotline on behalf of a Vietnam combat veteran given a debilitating series of eight electroshock treatments during a ten-day period in the VA hospital at North Chicago. Vetline-Hotline asked $150,000 damages in the suit, charging that the patient suffered permanent brain damage as a result of the treatments, which were carried out despite the absence of signed and written consent by the man's next of kin.

Psychiatrist Dr. Gilbert Bogen, the organization's president, has given high priority to a campaign to stop medical abuse, experimentation and mistreatment of veterans at VA hospitals. The work of Bogen and Vetline-Hotline led to efforts by Illinois legislators to regulate and protect veterans from being used as subjects for medical experiments in hospitals in the state. According to Dr. Bogen, "A list of medical experiments on humans at VA hospitals demonstrates that thousands of Illinois veterans are currently being used as research subjects." The former chief-of-staff at the VA hospital in North Chicago, Dr. Bogen claims to have collected official VA documents proving abuses to patients, some so grave that they resulted in death.

"The patients who are used for these research efforts are, like most VA consumers, individuals who have no alternative to medical care other than VA," he said. "Imagine the unspoken, and sometimes very obvious, pressures brought on these patients when they're asked to participate in an experiment. A lot of them say yes out of fear of being tossed out rather than any desire to become part of a research project."

Both Dr. Bogen and Philip H. Vision, Vetline-Hotline's national legislative coordinator, criticized the widespread use of medical students in the treatment of patients at veterans' hospitals, including unsupervised surgery by "doctors-in-training."

The beleaguered VA was also named as defendant in a suit that includes the Ryans as plaintiffs, and was handled by the National Veterans Law Center in Washington, D.C. Filed in U.S. District Court in the capital in 1979, the action challenges VA rules leading to denial of disability claims by veterans and family members for ailments related to exposure to Agent Orange in Vietnam. The veterans claimed that the VA had rejected hundreds of claims and refused to consider scientific data linking their health problems to the herbicides. Various other suits have been filed independently of the AOVI-sponsored action throughout the country.

The Ryans are anxious for a resolution of the muddled litigation so that they can obtain a cash settlement to be used for Kerry's needs, and to see other veterans and their families compensated for medical expenses and suffering. But they are insistent that there is a moral and criminal debt that must also be paid. They are firm about the need to publicly establish responsibility. "It's a moral issue, and I know we're gong to win because I believe in God and I know we're right and they're wrong," Michael says. "But they must be made to admit they're wrong." Michael and Maureen are convinced, as others are, that the chemical companies were aware of the carcinogenic and terato-genic qualities of 2,4,5-T years before it was dumped on American soldiers and on the ground where they fought in Vietnam. Consequently the responsibility for the death-and-mutilation-dealing poisons veterans carried home with them from Vietnam constitutes a criminal offense.

"Some of these executives from the chemical compa-nies belong in jail," Michael declares. "We have veterans and children who have spent years trying to cope with catastrophic disabilities without help. Now that we know who is responsible, we want help for the veterans and we want the people who sold them out to go to prison for it. They're criminals. They knew!"

Although the class-action megasuit filed against the war contractors does not provide for criminal penalties against the companies or against any individuals, a victory in court might well clear the way for later criminal pro-ceedings.

The gigantic suit was set up for trial in three phases—the first two to determine liability and harm to the plain-tiffs, and the third to establish the amount of damages. The final phase will be tried in local courts.

No one knows how long it may be before the legal maneuvering and maze of litigation is sorted out and the veterans and their families are able to end the limbo they must live in until that time. It could be years. And for many veterans, like Paul Reutershan, it is already too late.

10

TOMORROW

A baby is God's opinion that the world should go on. . . .
Carl Sandburg

In the middle of March 1981, Maureen pulled the Ryans' car into a parking space for the handicapped at the Stony Brook University Hospital near their home. She walked into the emergency entrance and returned with a wheel-chair for Kerry.

Mother and daughter were excited, yet anxious, over an appointment with an orthopedic specialist who did recon-structive work on limbs using sections of bone from cadavers. If Kerry was lucky, he might be able to use the technique to make her malformed arm more functional.

They waited three hours. Kerry's excited anticipation turned into apprehension, then fear. She had been in and out of hospitals all her life, and they held too many un-pleasant memories. She was terrified and pestering her mother to go home before they were finally led into an examining room. Trailed by a retinue of young residents, the surgeon walked inside, took one look at Kerry, and pronounced, "Thalidomide." Although the instant diag-nosis was wide of the mark, Maureen was struck by the surgeon's obvious recognition that Kerry's imperfect body was the result of chemical attack.

Examinations disclosed that Kerry could not be significantly helped by the new surgical technique. The examinations also disclosed that two other parts of her hand were missing, defects not previously noticed despite ten years of poking, prodding, testing and X-raying by some of the most capable pediatricians and orthopedic surgeons in the country. Maureen had heard worse news from doctors. Worse news was coming.

She was asked to hold Kerry in front of her and to help her walk. After a few moments, she helped Kerry turn so that the medical team could see her spine. "Scoliosis," one of the doctors murmured.

Maureen knew that the term was used to describe an abnormal curvature of the spine, but she had never before heard it used in relation to Kerry. She was also familiar with spinal bifida, a common birth defect among Agent Orange babies. As they were examining Kerry's spine after observing the scoliosis, the doctors learned that she also had an internal form of spinal bifida, and her sacrum and coccyx bones were missing.

Maureen was suddenly very tired. She realized that for Kerry, the war in Vietnam would never be over. She would carry her wounds and face new battles all her life.

"What do you do in this situation?" Maureen asked.

"Well, if you don't do something about it, you will greatly shorten her life," the surgeon advised.

Kerry was ten years old, and doctors were still talking as frankly in her presence as they had when she was an infant. She was taking in every word, and it frightened her. When she got home, it would be the job of her parents to calm her fears and to reassure her she wasn't going to die. They had done it before but not without some bitterness about the lack of concern by doctors for the apprehensions and nightmares of a little girl.

Driving home with Kerry riding silently beside her,

Maureen thought of how she would tell Michael that there had to be yet another dangerous operation. Revelation of each newly discovered birth defect hurt as deeply as had the first. Instead of eighteen birth defects, Kerry now had twenty-two. Maureen glanced at her daughter. In a body so tiny, how can so many things be so wrong, she wondered. The thoughts flooded through Maureen's mind, and she suddenly realized that it was March 19—exactly two years since she, Michael, and Kerry had joined in the class-action lawsuit filed by Yannacone.

Someday, when the suit has been settled, Mike and Maureen plan to buy a house and a van, both specially designed for their daughter. Most homes and most vehicles are not designed for the physically impaired, and they can too often become prisoners of their handicaps. The Ryans are determined not to permit that to happen to Kerry. Normal features of most homes, such as stairs and doorways too narrow to accommodate wheelchairs, constitute impossible barriers for Kerry. So Kerry will have a house of her own that has been built to accommodate her special needs.

Houses like the Ryans want for their daughter have been constructed for war-injured veterans like Bobby Muller. Kerry is a war-injured veteran, too. And when she moves from the cozy but unmanageable home in Stony Brook, it will be to a new ranch-style, single-level house with ramps and wide doorways designed to permit her entry by wheelchair into every room.

Attempting to improve Kerry's mobility and control of her environment, Maureen learned of a compact, easy-to-transport, battery-operated device resembling a golf cart that is called a Portascooter. Kerry was thrilled at the prospect of owning one when a salesman demonstrated the device for the family, but the Ryans' insurance carrier at first refused to pay the $1,500 cost, though they eventually agreed to pay after the Ryans made the decision public. Michael and Maureen's combined income was too high to qualify for any of the federal programs designed to assist low-income families with similar needs, despite the catastrophic drain on their finances by Kerry's treatment and care.

Kerry weighed eighty-five pounds when she was ten years old, and her leg braces added another thirty pounds of dead weight. She was already too heavy for her 124-pound mother to lift, and she is rapidly approaching the time when her father will be unable to carry her.

A properly designed home with ramps and a van equipped with a lift to hoist Kerry and her wheelchair inside would eliminate the need for carrying her anywhere around her home. A house built to the necessary specifications might cost $100,000. It would cost at least $25,000 to renovate the family's current home so that Kerry could move about more freely. A fully equipped, four-wheel-drive van, including a $3,000 hoist to lift her wheelchair inside and out, a radio, and an air conditioner would cost approximately $16,000 or $17,000. And the van would have to be replaced every four or five years.

The Ryans have wanted a van for Kerry since shortly after her motor abilities were damaged by the embolism, but the need was underscored in February 1978, when the car Maureen was driving became mired in snow on an isolated stretch of road during a blizzard. Kerry, with her frail health and susceptibility to pneumonia, was not with her mother that night. But Michael and Maureen later sat and talked with each other, wondering and fretting about what might have happened if she had been.

If Kerry had a van, her parents could use it for trips to the beach and drive across the sand until they found a secluded location for family outings. The four-wheel-drive vehicle would provide not only dependable transportation but privacy for Kerry's toilet needs as well. Kerry is protected by her family, but she will never be overprotected. And, although she will always be treasured, she will never be pampered. Her parents love her enough to demand that she achieve. They believe in expressing their love practically, as well as sentimentally.

Ironically Michael can no longer take full advantage of the beach as he once did. He was talking with Yannacone one day when the attorney noticed the mottled appearance of Michael's arms. The skin was dotted with tiny iridescent spots. "That's a sign of dioxin poisoning," Yannacone advised him. "It's deep cellular change, and too much sun can cause skin cancer." Consequently Michael, like Joan Maiman, has to take great care that he does not undergo long periods of exposure to sunlight. Denial of an opportunity to sun and swim along the miles of beaches bordering Long Island is just one more sacrifice that he has had to accept.

Michael's tour in Vietnam and his exposure to Agent Orange has left its mark on the Ryan family in many ways. If the house that his parents bought in Brookhaven ever fills with grandchildren, it will be the children of Michael's sisters and their husbands.

In 1979 Patty and her husband, Freddie Stransky, had been married for seven years. Kerry was nine years old, she had weathered the perilous operation on her heart, survived other threats on her life, and the family considered her to be sufficiently mature and healthy to share attention with a new baby. The Stranskys decided it was time to start their family. Patty became pregnant. Her husband remembered watching other men spray chemicals from backpacks, from trucks, and from aircraft when he was in Vietnam. It was conceivable that he, too, might have brought back traces of dioxin in his body to be passed on to a child, even though he exhibited none of the symptoms. There were so many mysterious factors surrounding the chemicals used in Vietnam, as well as the unknown chances of his exposure, that it was impossible to compute Freddie's odds for or against producing a healthy baby.

Patty's pregnancy was closely monitored. During the fifteenth week she submitted to a sonargram, which is an ultrasound scan of the mother's abdomen that produces an outline of the developing fetus on a screen. If signs indicated possible abnormal limb development, Patty was prepared to submit to amniocentesis or fetoscopy to further confirm the diagnosis.

Amniocentesis can detect chromosomal abnormalities in the fetus fifteen weeks after conception. It is seldom performed after sixteen weeks because of the danger associated with preventive abortion after so long a period of development, if serious abnormalities are perceived. The prenatal diagnostic technique is accomplished by insertion of a hollow needle into the womb and withdrawal of about an ounce of the amniotic fluid, which contains living and dead cells that have naturally separated from the fetus. The fluid is incubated for three weeks in a laboratory, then examined.

Fetoscopy is usually carried out between the fifteenth and twentieth weeks of pregnancy and permits direct examination of the fetus. Utilizing high-frequency sound waves for guidance, a fine apparatus containing an optical lens is inserted through a small incision in the abdomen to permit viewing. Samples of the blood and tissue may also be extracted for laboratory examination.

Despite her Roman Catholic background, Patty decided to have an abortion if the tests indicated an imperfectly developed fetus. And if, after all the precautions, she gave birth to a baby with serious congenital defects, she and Freddie had decided that they would not sign papers permitting operations to prolong its life.

Kevin Michael Stransky was born on June 24, 1980. He weighed seven pounds, was healthy, and had no apparent birth defects. Kevin's healthy birth was a cause for celebration. Their emotions and hopes were high. Another afflicted baby would have been a devastating blow.

Deirdre and her husband, Walter Stransky, were nevertheless still postponing plans to begin a family as of this writing. Walter served eighteen months of duty in Vietnam with the U.S. Coast Guard and was based in the heavily sprayed delta area.

Although they are looking optimistically toward the future, the Ryans and the Stranskys cannot ignore the past. Vietnam will not be forgotten, and Agent Orange is part of a deadly legacy and common link they share with the families of other veterans. Maureen longs to have another child, a brother or sister for Kerry, "a child who is easy this time." But there will be no second child for the Ryans.

Most veterans still consider themselves to be patriots, as they did when they trooped to Indochina to fight their country's unpopular war. And when they complain, it is because they have given so much of themselves and they expect the country they served so honestly to give with honesty in return.

A new study showed that the incidence of wife and child abuse among the 8.5 million veterans who served during the hostilities in Vietnam was higher than that of other men in their age group who did not serve in the military. The rates of abuse were higher for those who served in Vietnam, and higher yet for those who were in combat.

Suicide rates for veterans of the Vietnam war also exceeded the rates for nonveterans. A study conducted for the General Counsel for the House Armed Services Committee disclosed early in 1981 that more Vietnam veterans committed suicide after discharge than the number of the American soldiers who died in the war. David Christian, the most highly decorated American soldier of the conflict, said in Philadelphia at the opening of a national veterans' pilot job program, that more than 50,000 veterans had died by their own hands since their return from Indochina. Some 57,207 were listed as killed in action between 1965 and January 1973.

In March 1981 a thirty-two-year-old Marine veteran dressed in green jungle camouflage fatigues crashed his jeep through the glass doors of the Wadsworth VA hospital in Los Angeles, shooed away a half dozen people, and sprayed the lobby with gunfire. No one was injured, although James Hopkins was reportedly armed with five loaded guns and had fired fourteen shots while screaming that he had been exposed to Agent Orange and no one cared. Then he opened a can of beer and waited for police to arrive.

Hopkins was arraigned on charges of destroying federal property, then freed on $25,000 bail pending trial in July. He complained that he had suffered intermittent ringing in his ears after returning from Vietnam in 1969. A VA physician examined him and diagnosed irreparable nerve damages in the right ear and progressive hearing loss in the other, he said. But he charged that the VA refused to admit the full extent of his hearing loss.

Two months after the VA hospital was shot up, Hopkins's wife, Suzanne, returned to their home and found him dying in bed. An empty bottle of pills and a partly full bottle of bourbon were beside him. There was no suicide note, and coroner's investigators termed the initial results of the autopsy inconclusive.

Indiscriminate dumping of toxic wastes is polluting waterways and housing developments, chemical spray is spreading airborne poison over pastures and forest, and exhaust from automobiles and factories is making smog synonymous with life in American cities. Pollution and chemical poison are becoming a national tragedy.

One survey by the EPA pinpointed more than 30,000 dumps around the country that are filled with dangerous, difficult-to-eradicate chemical waste. Legislators are debating creation of a superfund to pay for a nationwide cleanup, which it is estimated may cost as much as $50 billion. One proposal in Washington suggested that the chemical companies pay seventy-five percent of the cost and that the federal government assume the remaining twenty-five percent. The suggestion for a chemical waste cleanup superfund was rejected out-of-hand by the industry. Chemical Manufacturers' Association President Robert Roland insisted that: "There is no need for a superfund bill. If all society has benefitted from the jobs and the products of the chemical industry, then the risks should also be spread across the whole society."*

Families like those chased from their homes by the poisonous wastes dumped at the Love Canal, or the Robert Ralstons of Arkansas whose health and cattle business were broken by straying airborne herbicidal spray, would undoubtedly find much to argue with in Roland's references to the "benefits" of the poisons produced by the chemical industry. People in almost every state have personal horror stories of the ecological and human disasters wreaked by careless manufacture, use, and disposal of toxic chemicals.

Tennessee Congressman Albert Gore, presiding at hearings on the burgeoning problem of hazardous wastes, credited the tragedy of the Love Canal with awakening

---

*January 3, 1980, *Washington Post*, by Joan Omag.

the public to the link between health problems and chemicals. He predicted that ". . . as the public becomes more aware, there's going to be a solution."

A government study conducted for the eighteen-agency Toxic Substances Strategy Committee disclosed in 1980 that the cancer rate in the U.S. was increasing and that toxic chemicals may be a factor in twenty percent of all cases.

Dr. Joseph Hightower, a spokesman for the Environmental Defense Fund, observed that the search for a cancer cure must be connected to the problem of chemical waste. "Now most scientists agree that the overwhelming majority of cancers are chemically caused," he said. Some scientists believe that as much as ninety percent of all cancer may be caused by environmental factors, including chemical waste.

Veterans exposed to toxic substances in Vietnam already know how serious the problem of contamination by toxic chemicals is. It is life threatening—and baby crippling. This is the chemical age, nevertheless, and it is up to society to determine if the substances isolated or developed in laboratories and factories will become molecules of progress or of human destruction. The same chemicals that have enriched our lives and spurred agricultural production by providing medicines, plastics, and insecticides through carelessness or misuse have also been responsible for the Love Canal and the poisoning of Americans in Vietnam. The Vietnamese, of course, have suffered and will continue to suffer horribly from prolonged chemical attack on their people and habitat.

It may be that the chemical-related health problems of Vietnam veterans and their children will eventually be solved in the country where it started. Although working with facilities which are primitive by American standards, large-scale studies are being carried out in Vietnam on the effects of the dioxin-contaminated herbicides. In Vietnam there is no longer any reason to attempt to cover up or to deny the damaging effect of the toxins on human health and reproduction.

Veterans like Michael Ryan, Johnny Woods, Frank McCarthy, and their wives are aware of the need for further scientific inquiry into the damaging properties of the dioxin and the arsenic laden chemicals unleashed on Vietnam and on the soldiers who served there. But veterans and their families need help now. It is too late for parades, and too late to wait until lengthy new studies have satisfied every industrialist, bureaucrat, and scientist. Kerry Ryan is growing up. She outgrows a pair of $1,000 braces every year. She needs a lightweight battery-powered wheelchair or Portascooter, a lift-equipped van, and a ranch-style home with ramps. Soon she will have to undergo surgery again on her spine. And before very long, she will have to be operated on for removal of her duplicate reproductive organs. Kerry and children like her need hours of therapy with well-trained and expensive specialists who can help extract every ounce of their potential as human beings and to equip them to participate as fully as possible in the activities of their peers.

Young veterans like Reutershan are dying. They cannot, and must not, be expected to wait two years, ten years, or even one more year for help while more veterans die and more children are born dead or with calamitous abnormalities. It is misplaced concern to worry about the billions of dollars in tax money and in profits from the powerful petrochemical industry needed to treat, to care for, and to provide monetary compensation for the terrible damage done to veterans and their families.

The men and women responded when their country called them. Now it is time for their country to respond to their call.

SELECTED BIBLIOGRAPHY

BOOKS

Berger, Carl, ed. *The United States Air Force in Southeast Asia.* Washington, D.C.: Office of Air Force History, 1977.

Brown, Michael. *Laying Waste: The Poisoning of America by Toxic Chemicals.* New York: Panthcon, 1980.

Carson, Rachel. *Silent Spring.* Boston: Houghton Mifflin, 1962.

Ensign, Tod, and Michael Uhl. *GI Guinea Pigs: How the Pentagon Exposed Our Troops to Dangers More Deadly Than War.* New York: Playboy Press, 1980.

Fuller, John G. *The Poison That Fell From the Sky.* New York: Random House, 1977.

Hersh, Seymour. *Chemical and Biological Warfare: America's Hidden Arsenal.* Indianapolis: Bobbs-Merrill, 1968.

Middleton, Drew "Introduction". *Air War—Vietnam.* New York: Arno Press, 1978.

Rose, Steven. *CBW Chemical and Biological Warfare.* Boston: Beacon Press, 1969.

Schlesinger, Arthur M. *A Thousand Days: John F. Kennedy In The White House,* Boston: Houghton Mifflin, 1965.

Starry, Gen. Donn A. *Mounted Combat in Vietnam.* Washington, D.C.: Department of the Army, 1978.

Whiteside, Thomas. *Defoliation: What Are Our Herbicides Doing To Us?* New York: Ballantine/Friends of the Earth, 1970.

Whiteside, Thomas. *The Pendulum and the Toxic Cloud: The Course of Dioxin Contamination.* New Haven: Yale University Press, 1979.

Whiteside, Thomas. *The Withering Rain: America's Herbicidal Folly.* New York: E. P. Dutton & Company, 1971.

MAGAZINES, PAMPHLETS, PAPERS

Agent Orange Victims International. "Agent Orange Fact Sheet: A Historical Perspective." New York: undated.

Agent Orange Victims International Newsletter. New York: 1980.

Allen, J. R., Barsoti, D. A., Van Miller, J. P., Abrahamson, L. J., and Lalich, J. J. "Morphological Changes in Monkeys Concerning a Diet Containing Low Levels of 2,3,7,8 Tetrachlorodibenzo-p-Dioxin." Department of Pathology, University of Wisconsin, Madison, Wisconsin, April 1, 1977.

Barnet, Anthony, and Mike Goldwater. "Wouldn't Hurt a Mouse." *New Statesman* (August 22, 1980).

Bionetics Research Laboratories. "Evaluation of Carcinogenic, Teratogenic and Mutagenic Activities of Selected Pesticides and Industrial Chemicals." Study for National Cancer Institute. National Technical Information Service. Three Volumes.

Boffey, Philip M. "Defense Issues Summary of Defoliation Study." *Science* (February 9, 1968), p. 613.

Browne, Corinne. "The Vietnam Veteran: Vets in Prison." *Penthouse* (July 1974), pp. 57–63.

Commoner, Dr. Barry, and R. F. Scott. "U. S. Air Force Studies on the Stability and Ecological Effects of TCDD (Dioxin): An Evaluation Relative to the Accidental Dissemination of TCDD At Seveso, Italy." Washington University, St. Louis, Missouri, 1976.

Daschle, Congressman Tom. "Herbicide Agent Orange."

Opening statement before the Subcommittee on Medical Facilities and Benefits of the Committee on Veterans Affairs, House of Representatives. July 22, 1980.

Galston, Arthur W. "Implications of the Widespread Use of Herbicides." *Bioscience* 21, no. 14, pp. 891–92.

General Accounting Office of the Comptroller General. *Health Effects of Exposure to Herbicide Orange in South Vietnam Should Be Resolved.* Washington, D.C.: April 10, 1979.

————. *U.S. Ground Troops in South Vietnam Were in Areas Sprayed with Herbicide Orange.* Washington, D.C.: November 16, 1979.

General Accounting Office. Report to Congressman Ralph H. Metcalf on: (1) "The Extent of Defense Use of Herbicides and Other Chemicals in Vietnam." (2) "The Number of Military and Civilian Personnel Exposed to These Chemicals." (3) "The Defense-Funded Studies of the Health Effects of These Chemicals." August 16, 1978; transcript of hearing on "Herbicide 'Agent Orange.'" Subcommittee on Medical Facilities and Benefits of the Committee on Veterans Affairs, U.S. House of Representatives. October 11, 1978.

Helmer, John. "Bringing the War Home, The American Soldier in Vietnam and After." New York: The Free Press, 1974.

Hornblower, Margot. "Herbicide, Birth Defects Linked for House Panel." *Washington Post* (June 22, 1979), p. A8.

Johnson, Julius E. "The Public Health Implications of Widespread Use of Phenoxy Herbicides and Picolaram." *Bioscience* 21, pp. 899–904.

Kidder, Tracy. "Soldiers of Misfortune." *The Atlantic* (March 1978), pp. 41–89.

Kroger, William. "Whatever Happened to the Vietnam Veteran?: Today, Most of Them Have Settled Down to a Job, a Home, and a Family." *Nation's Business* (December, 1978), pp. 74–77.

Kurtis, Bill. "Burnt Orange." *The New York Times* (March 18, 1980), p. A23.

Mathews, Jay. "Vietnam Veterans Esteemed in Korea." *Washington Post* (July 2, 1980), pp. A-1 and A-21.

Meselson, Matthew S. "Chemical and Biological Weapons." *Scientific American* 222, no. 5, pp. 15–25.

Meselson, Matthew S., and P. W. O'Keefe. "Human Milk Monitoring: Preliminary Results for Twenty-One Samples." The Biological Laboratories, Harvard University, December 15, 1976.

Miller, Alan S. "Health." *Environment* 21, no. 5, pp. 2–4.

Mrak, E. M., ed. "Report of the Secretary's Commission on Pesticides and Their Relationship to Environmental Health." United States Department of Health, Education and Welfare. 1969.

National Academy of Science/National Research Council. "The Effects of Herbicides in South Vietnam." 1974.

National Academy of Science. *The Effects of Herbicides in South Vietnam, Part A, Summary and Conclusions.* Washington, D.C.: 1974.

Neilands, Orions, Pfeiffer, Vennema and Westing. "Harvest of Death, Chemical Warfare in Viet-Nam and Cambodia." New York: The Free Press, 1972.

Payne, Karen J. "Beyond Vietnam, Beyond Politics, Beyond Causes . . ." *Barrister.* Young Lawyers Association, Chicago. Volume 6, Number 2. pp 10–14 and 52. Spring, 1979.

Penthouse. "The Vietnam Veterans Advisor." (January 1979), p. 118.

Penthouse. "The Vietnam Veterans Advisor." (August 1980), p. 102.

Peracchio, Adrian. "2 From LI Describe Agent Orange Horror." *Newsday* (June 27, 1979).

Richardson, David B. "Seveso—One Year Later. The Continuing Agony of a Town Buried in Industrial Poison." *U.S. News & World Report* (August 1, 1977), pp. 44–45.

Severo, Richard. "Two Crippled Lives Mirror Disputes on Herbicides." First article in three-part series entitled "Legacy of Suspicion." *The New York Times* (May 27, 1979), p. A-1.

———. "U.S. Disputes Claims of Veterans, Says None are Herbicide Victims." *The New York Times* (May 28, 1979), p. A-1.

———. "Herbicides Pose a Bitter Mystery in U.S. Decades after Discovery." *The New York Times* (May 29, 1979), p. A-1.

Smith, Jeffrey R. "Dioxins Have Been Present Since the Advent of Fire, Says Dow." *Science* 202 (December 15, 1978), pp. 1166–67.

Tarbell, Marta. "The Agent Orange Time Bomb." *Penthouse* (August 1979), pp. 75–114.

Veterans Administration. "Worried About Agent Orange?" (July 1, 1980.) Informational folder. Veterans Administration. Washington, D.C.

Vetline-Hotline. "Vetline News." Highland Park, Illinois.

Westing, Arthur. "Ecological Effects of Military Defoliation in the Forests of South Vietnam." *Bioscience* 21, no. 17, pp. 873–98.

Yannacone, Victor John, Jr. "Ecologically Sophisticated, Environmentally Responsible, Socially Relevant, and Politically Feasible Legislation." *Leadership 70* (December 12, 1969). Midwinter Republican Governors Conference. Hot Springs, Arkansas.

———. "Environment and the Law," in *Environment: Resources, Pollution and Society,* edited by William

Murdoch. Stamford, Connecticut: Sinauer Associates, Inc., 1971.

Zwerdling, Daniel. "The Immolation of Agent Orange." *New Times* (August 5, 1977), pp. 13–14.

APPENDIX A

TESTIMONY OF CHRISTOPHER H. JOHNSON
TO SUBCOMMITTEE ON MEDICAL
FACILITIES AND BENEFITS
July 22, 1980

Mr. Chairman, I am privileged to appear before the Veterans Affairs Subcommittee on Medical Facilities and Benefits to discuss the devastating effects and problems the Vietnam Veterans are dealing with on a daily basis.

At nineteen, I was a machine gunner on an armored personnel carrier with the Eleventh Armored Cavalry. I served in Tay Ninh Province, which was heavily concentrated with herbicides. At nineteen, I was killing people for what I naively believed in. In March of 1970, I lost my right leg and sustained multiple fragment wounds to my left foot, left hip, right arm, and also have a hearing loss, all due to a confrontation with the North Vietnamese Army. I spent thirteen months at Fitzsimmons Army Hospital in Denver.

Ten years later, I find that while I was fighting for what I believed in, government agencies were experimenting with us and everything around. Today, I can no longer be the naive person I was at nineteen years old. I can still be a patriot, but I cannot approve of some of my country's thoughtless actions. You took the cream of the crop for that war; look around you today, look at what has been done to that crop. The hard-fighting men that were in Vietnam are withering away like the defoliated Vietnam.

While I was in Vietnam, I had a respiratory problem which I reported to the medical unit. Unsurprisingly to me, it is not in my medical records. I still have reoccurring respiratory problems. When I was at Fitzsimmons, I very vividly remember the chloracne-like retention cysts that I developed. I remember other patients lying around pulling them out of their arms and legs. I still have this embarrassing problem. At that time, we made no connection.

About three years ago, I weighed 175 pounds; a short time later I weighed 130 pounds after having intestinal problems, loss of appetite, and flu-type symptoms which I still have. I went to doctors at the VA and the Air Force only to have them say nothing was wrong and send me home. Not once did they mention Agent Orange. I had to tell them and show them an article in December of 1979.

During my weight loss, we conceived our second child. Nicholas was born with chromosome damage, which they tested my wife and I for with negative results. Nicholas had every imaginable deformity, about twenty-six in all. To list a few: club feet, deformed hands and face, a hole in his heart, his intestines were outside of his body along with his liver, cysts on his kidneys, etc. My wife and I believe in natural childbirth, so I was present in the delivery room. When he was delivered, the nurse said, "Hurry, get the doctor," to the other nurse. Nicholas was flown 400 miles to Denver to try to save him. What a blessing he is not here today to struggle for life as many Vietnam Veterans' children do. When I go to the VA hospital, the only way to get there is to go past the National Cemetery, where my son is buried. What a strange feeling to know my son is also a victim of war. The doctors cannot explain why, they only say he is the worst case they have seen as they send me the medical bills.

I have started Vietnam Veterans of South Dakota to work with all the other service organizations, such as the DAV, VFW, American Legion, and the Vietnam Veterans organizations. The South Dakota DAV is covering my expenses out here so I can help represent us. We are all working with veterans, helping them where the VA has failed. We are reaching out to them and letting them know someone is there who cares and will not label them a hypochondriac, because my symptoms are just as real as theirs. We let them know what to expect on an Agent Orange exam at the VA. Many veterans think they will find out if chemicals are ruining their bodies. Many find out that they are subjected to a questionnaire of nonsensible questions. Also, the VA Central Office [VACO] sent out memos to hospitals instructing them to only give simple reassurance that their problems are not connected to herbicides and also to make no relationship between the veterans' symptoms and Agent Orange in their medical records. It's working. They put it that way in my records.

How can the VACO even expect to learn from the Agent Orange exam registry about our problems when the VACO instructs the local VA to discredit what a veteran complains of?

The United States sent these same questionnaires to the Repatriation Commission in Australia for their use on veterans over there. They discontinued its use because of the complaints about the questions. They report the same exact symptoms along with the same birth defects. But yet the U.S. government agencies and Australia are trading information so that they can keep on trying to discredit all veterans' claims.

In Australia at Sydney's Royal Alexandria Hospital for Children, Dr. David Walsh, a biochemist on fetal deformities, said regarding limb deformities, "Something stinks. There is obviously something wrong. At this stage we can't say whether it is linked with Agent Orange, but to say that there is no scientific evidence showing a link is to say nothing. It just plain means we haven't done the work." Dr. Walsh examined veterans' children free of charge. Their complaints are identical to ours.

You can no longer look the other way. Our health problems are real and won't go away just as we won't go away. The men who fought in Vietnam joined in brotherhood because then it was survival that brought us together; today, it is survival again.

April 15, 1970, the Surgeon General appeared before the Energy Subcommittee and announced governmental actions aimed at limiting the use of 2,4,5-T in the United States. The same day the Deputy Secretary of Defense, David Packard, announced that the military would stop using Agent Orange in Vietnam. With those actions, doesn't that tell you that the risks were greater than the benefits?

Also, during 1970, the chemical companies were fighting the Department of Agriculture to keep the use of 2,4,5-T on rice crops on the grounds that it brought larger food yields. At the same time, in 1970, the military used this chemical to destroy one-half million acres of rice crops on Vietnam. Doesn't this tell you that the severe concentrations used in Vietnam were harmful?

In pointing out concentrations, I make reference to Army TM 3-216, page 74, Section III 107, dated 1964. "These compounds are effective in killing plants when used in concentrations as low as 0.5 pounds per acre. This concentration is generally nontoxic to man and animals. There are no proven defensive measures against these compounds. By the time symptoms appear, nothing can be done to prevent damage."

In reference to the Minnesota Department of Veterans Affairs Study, Section II Application procedures used in

South Vietnam: "Agent Orange was sprayed undiluted at
the rate of three gallons per acre (12 pounds of 2,4-D and
13.8 pounds of 2,4.5-T per acre.)" That is 13.3 pounds per
acre more than the Army manual recommended. The
Herbs Tapes show that some areas were sprayed as much
as twenty-five times in just a few short months. Doesn't
that sound very harmful to human health at such heavy
concentrations? On one occasion there were 1,000 gallons
dumped on a delegation office.

If Agent Orange is so nontoxic to us, why then did the
Air Force draft an Environmental Impact Statement on
how to get rid of existing stocks of Agent Orange without
danger to human health or the environment?

If it is no threat to man, why then in February of 1972
did the Mississippi Air and Pollution Control Commission
request that Agent Orange be removed from storage at
Gulfport, Mississippi, immediately?

The USAF OEHL Technical Report, TR-78-92, page
1-2, table 4, Acres Treated shows that between 1967
and 1969 were the years when the most acres were
treated.

The Agent Orange organizations that are taking questionnaires are finding that most of the men complaining
of health problems served during 1967 and 1970. That
should show some relationship. Isn't it odd how the lay-
man can find disturbing similarities? Yet part of the scientific community cannot? Maude DeVictor is a layperson
who could see a relationship among men and their service
in Vietnam. I find it very hard to believe that anyone
could write such an accurate memo without help from
someone in the scientific community.

Referring back to the USAF OEHL report, page 1–3: In
April, 1970, the Secretaries of Agriculture, Health, Education and Welfare and the Interior jointly announced the
suspension of certain uses of 2,4,5-T. These suspensions

resulted from studies published indicating that 2,4,5-T was a teratogen.

It also appears that Vietnam was a proving ground for herbicides. From the same report page I-2 and I-3, Brown reported "that the first shipments of Herbicides Purple and Blue was received in Vietnam the 9th of January, 1962." Also, the report says, "Two additional phenoxy herbicide formulations were received in Vietnam in limited quantities and evaluated during the first two years of Operation Ranch Hand." These were Pink and Green. Then, in 1965, two more were brought in: Orange and White. Orange replaced Purple, Pink, and Green. The Air Force also conducted an experiment in Vietnam along with the National Forestry Department called Pink Rose. Pink Rose was an operation where Orange and Blue were applied to kill off an area of vegetation followed with a burning-off process.

If TCDD is the result of a heating process, then it is possible that there was a lot of smoke filled with TCDD around from this and other fires.

In 1977 the World Health Organization's International Agency for Research on Cancer studied research papers going back twenty years. Their results indicated that TCDD could create serious health effects on humans:

Dermatological Chloracne: a severe skin disease of follicular and sebaceous glands, causing skin lesions, sebaceous cysts, blisters and pustules, and eventual scaring of the skin. Susceptibility to bruising, hyperpigmentation of the skin, and abnormal body hair growth.

Internal Liver damage: inflamed tissues, fatty changes, specialized cell degeneration, abnormal liver function, disorders of fat metabolism, disorders of carbohydrate metabolism. Heart and blood vessel disorders. Urinary tract disorders. Respiratory disorders. Pancreatic disorders.

Neurological   Polyneuropathies: a number of disease conditions of the nervous sytem. There may be polyneuritis, abdominal pain, and mental disturbance. Lower extremity weakness. Sensorial impairments—sight, hearing, smell, and taste.

Psychiatric   Depressive syndromes: a state of general debility, both physical and mental.

(Taken from: World Health Organization, International Agency for Research on Cancer. Monographs on the Evaluation of the Carcinogenic Risk of Chemicals to Man. Volume 15. Lyon, France: August 1977.)

The Armed Forces Institute of Pathology (AFIP) [had a monthly report from August 15, 1979,] on cases submitted from veterans and labeled "Possible Exposure to Herbicides During the Vietnam War." Page 4.

Of particular interest are the following:
(1)   unusual or unique tumors occurring in an organ or organ system.
(2)   an unusually high incidence of a tumor for a particular anatomic site.
(3)   a tumor occurring at an unusually young age.

(This was included in the VACO Steering Committee minutes on Herbicide Toxicity, November 15, 1979.)

Why doesn't the VA print some of these results in their Public Opinion Digest? Instead, they print about everything they can find to sour the VA staff on the Agent Orange issue. This type of one-sided point of view affects the staff all the way down to the scheduling workers that greet you at the front doors. If you insist that the jury is still out on the Agent Orange issue, then what do you think this type of publicating [*sic*] does to affect the veteran seeking medical attention?

In an Air Force report by Young and Thalken was the following: Table 16

Number of Fetuses Found per Female Mouse in Test and Control Areas

year of capture	# of fetuses control group I	# of fetuses test group II	% diff. groups I & II
1973	2.4	1.4	−46.6%
1974	1.1	0.7	−36.4%

But yet Young and Thalken concluded "TCDD encountered in the field failed to induce observable developmental defects."

You can clearly see that like Barry Commoner and Robert E. Scott of the Center for the Biology of Natural Systems point out in their evaluation, "the Air Force data include striking evidence of either a decline in fertility or an increase in fetal deaths in the TCDD exposed mouse population."

There are many animal tests in the scientific community that show numerous health effects and fetal problems. Such laboratory testing is usually accepted. It seems that many do not want to accept these results concerning herbicides. Are we going to wait for another body count of men who fought in the Vietnam War?

It is easy to see why no one will own up to the fact that we were overexposed to chemicals that are harming our health. First of all, the chemical companies have too much to lose since they depend so much on all the revenue that they receive. As an example: Dow Chemical's sales of agricultural chemicals was $398 million in 1978, and $471 million in 1979, the majority of it being herbicides. There are chemical plants worldwide, including Australia. If the Australian government were to decide that their men were seriously affected, then that would set a precedent for us in the United States or vice versa. Some members in the timber industry think they could not live without its use also. It seems the thought pattern is that it would cost too many dollars. Does this mean I am still naive in believing human life is far more precious than money?

What does the veteran end up with? We wonder what happened to the phrase "life, liberty and the pursuit of happiness." The suffering men who were once healthy and fighting hard battles are now fighting the hardest battle of all, life. Now we say, "liberty, little happiness and the pursuit of life."

In conclusion, I must give you some of my very deep feelings, but these feelings apply to almost every veteran, especially those of us who face life-threatening health problems from chemical exposure.

We are the men who went to fight a very complicated war, and the suffering and dying was just as real as in all wars. You asked us to go and we went. We are the ones who were fighting on foreign soil so we could keep the United States such a freedom-loving country. You must not turn your backs on us now that we are in real need of help. We are not the ones who went to Canada for a while, who were allowed to come back home with a guaranteed work program. They are the men that you see smiling and healthy today. We are the men who made this country such a great place . . . along with the other war veterans. You are not turning your backs on the Vietnamese refugees or the Cuban refugees. You are still sending monetary aid to Vietnam and allowing Cubans to take up bed spaces in VA hospitals. I do not mind them coming to our country. I would in no way want to live in their countries either.

Don't you think it is only right to take care of the American men who supported you, first? We are natural-born citizens of the United States of America. We have been reaching out for years for help. Now is the time for you to step forward and take the responsibility and appropriate action. Don't leave us with the only benefit remaining, which is the burial benefit. A lot of Vietnam veterans have already used it much too early in life. The Vietnam veteran never had the chance to enjoy growing into healthy adulthood. Now I can't enjoy growing old. The evidence and facts have been in for years: Agent Orange is a killer.

APPENDIX B

Testimony before U.S. Senate Committee on Veterans Affairs, by Maureen Ryan, wife of Vietnam veteran Michael F. Ryan, and by Frank McCarthy, National Chairman of Agent Orange Victims International. Hon. Alan Cranston, Chairman.

Mrs. Ryan: Senator Cranston, my name is Maureen Ryan. My husband, Michael, is a Vietnam veteran who served honorably in the United States Army from November of 1965 to August of 1967. Four years after returning from Vietnam, Michael and I gave birth to our first and only child, Kerry, who was born with eighteen birth defects.

Since infancy, Michael and I were taught that the United States is not only the greatest country in the history of the world, but a country blessed by God, a country to be defended, if need be, with your last drop of blood. I was taught this by my father, a World War II veteran, who was awarded the Bronze Star on the beaches of Normandy and again later in the Battle of the Bulge. Michael was taught this by his father, again a World War II veteran, who is a veteran of five invasions with Douglas MacArthur in the Pacific.

My husband Michael is a Vietnam veteran, a disabled Vietnam veteran, and a police officer for the last ten years in Suffolk County. Michael is tremendously like both of Kerry's grandfathers. He is fiercely proud of his country, his service to this country, and the men who died and fought for this country. But just as surely as the bullets and bombs killed on the battlefields in Vietnam, maiming thousands of our men, Agent Orange has come home from those battlefields with our men. It has come home to maim and to kill additional thousands of men who naively thought they made it home safely. It would have been tragic enough if it had ended there.

But what the United States and what our Vietnam veterans did not know was that they carried home a tremendous legacy with them. They did not know that genetically on those battlefields were their children. So Agent Orange is now reaping an additional harvest of birth defects and cancers in our children and the men. We are losing our children through spontaneous abortions, through miscarriages, and perhaps most tragically in the surviving children with the horrifying birth defects.

So now the veterans—they cry from their graves, the sick cry from their wheelchairs and their deathbeds. And, most of all, our deformed children cry from their wheelchairs. They are crying for the recognition that they have the right to be treated with the same dignity and the same care in the VA system as Max Cleland himself was treated.

By opening the VA hospitals to these men and to their children, you will be reaffirming what our fathers taught us and what we will continue to teach our children. You will reaffirm that this is a country that is blessed by God, a country to be defended no matter what the cost.

I listened this morning to Max Cleland make a statement that, if the United States government and, in particular, if the Veterans Administration, would send out letters to all the 2.4 million Vietnam veterans, they would be too frightened, that the overwhelming response of the veteran would be to be shaken; that, if the United States government is saying, "Come into the VA hospital for testing," that we would not be able to stand the pressure, that we would completely fall apart. He made the statement after a woman, whom I have never met before, stood up. She was eight months pregnant. I feel that Max Cleland is insulting our intelligence, firstly, as we are adults. It is not frightening when you are handed knowledge. It is much more frightening when you are kept in the dark. It is much more frightening to give birth to a child with birth defects. It is much more frightening to know your husband is dying of cancer. I would welcome a letter from the VA. I would welcome the hospitals to be opened. Open hospitals but removed to VA abuses. Open hospitals and show this world that, if we are going to enter into another crisis, as we are in Afghanistan, we have to finish up the Vietnam War. We have to return dignity to these men. We have to defend and stand up for these children. You have to remember, with the children that I am speaking of, none of them are brain-damaged. None of them are retarded. They were born into horrendously deformed bodies and they have to face this the rest of their lives. Don't cripple their minds. Let's open these hospitals, let's give them top-rate care. Let's open the hospitals to the condition at the end of World War II. Let's give the veteran the same dignity that was afforded him by Omar Bradley. Let's make the VA hospitals the greatest teaching institution in the country. Let other nations in this world look to us and say, "When they send men to war, if they come home and their bodies are broken, we will not only take care of their bodies, we will take care of their minds."

Thank you.

Just one more thing. I had mentioned this morning I met a woman for the first time . . . who was eight months pregnant. This is the woman here; her name is Anna Frye. And I think she had the right, at the beginning of her pregnancy, to know about Agent Orange. I think she had the right to make a conscious decision on the information present, whether or not she wanted to become pregnant. She shouldn't be sitting here at eight months pregnant with four weeks to go with the sword of Agent Orange hanging both over her and her child's head. We owe her too much. We owe the child that she is carrying too much. This child is a future citizen. You've got to open your arms and welcome these people.

Thank you.

Chairman Cranston: Thank you very much for a superb statement. I appreciate it very deeply; very, very deeply. . . .

Mrs. Ryan: Senator Cranston?

Chairman Cranston: Yes?

Mrs. Ryan: The echo of pain that you are hearing in this room may come off as a tremendous amount of bitterness. I don't know whether bitterness is the right word so much as it is the level of frustration that has been reached. I think these people have lived private hells, and I don't think we would all be sitting here today if we didn't believe in this country. What we are saying, though, is that the government is the people and the government has to stand behind us.

Chairman Cranston: Thank you very much. . . .

Frank McCarthy is introduced:

Chairman Cranston: What is your understanding of the use of dioxin presently inside this country:

Mr. McCarthy: Inside this country?

Chairman Cranston: Yes, now.

Mr. McCarthy: It's not very—It's horrendous, I mean, to be perfectly straight out. Let's put it really on the table. Now hexachlorophene, years ago—Do you know about hexachlorophene, Senator?

Chairman Cranston: Yes.

Mr. McCarthy: We used to brush our teeth with it, wash our clothes with it, wash our bodies with Dial Soap and Phisohex. That is the same material, same chemical, that was used in the Seveso, Italy, plant that blew up and contaminated forty-five square acres, never to be used again by humans in Seveso, Italy.

Chairman Cranston: On the specific issue of dioxin, what is your understanding of its present use inside the United States?

Mr. McCarthy: The EPA has just banned, on March 2nd, seventy-five percent of the use. Now it is still being sprayed on the rice crops and the ranchlands, so I don't eat rice anymore.

Mrs. Ryan: Excuse me. I would just like to interject something when Frank said about all the rice crops. Presently, down in Arkansas, there is a plant by the name of Vertak, which is leaking dioxin. They found it outside the plant in the bayous, in the creeks. And Arkansas is our shellfish, so that will give you an idea of the contamination . . . .

APPENDIX C

DIRECTORY OF THE
VETERANS LEADERSHIP CONFERENCE
300 North State Street
Apartment 3409
Chicago, Illinois 60610

MEMBERS AND SUPPORTERS
November, 1980

Agent Orange Womens Support Group
4316 Nutmeg Lane
Lisle, Illinois 60532
Cheryl Koehler, R.N.
(Counsel women who are related to Agent Orange victims.)

American GI Forum
10550 Torrence Avenue
Chicago, Illinois 60617
Joseph Neri
(Counseling and employment referral.)

California Vietnam Veterans
57 Water Street
Pittsburg, California 94565
Pete Tiffany
(Counseling and support for Vietnam veterans.)

CAVEAT, Inc.
4316 Nutmeg Lane
Lisle, Illinois 60532
Mike Skyer, Ron DeYoung
(Information and action on Agent Orange.)

Central Pennsylvania Concerned Vietnam
Veterans Association
Rd. 1, PO Box 72
Parksburg, Pennsylvania 19365
Ken Dohner
(Services to Vietnam veterans.)

Disabled American Veterans—Member
536 South Clark Street
Chicago, Illinois 60605
Robert Valaski
(Services to eligible veterans.)

Drop-In Center
51 Clifton Avenue, Number 62101
Newark, New Jersey 07104
James Credle
(Assistance for discharge upgrade and incarcerated veterans.)

Goodwill Industries
120 South Ashland Boulevard
Chicago, Illinois 60607
Mrs. Shirley Morley
(Vocational rehabilitation training.)

Illinois Vietnam Veterans Civic Council
4316 Nutmeg Lane
Lisle, Illinois 60532
Michael Skyer
(Advise VA on Vietnam era matters.)

Kane County Veterans Association
Kane County Courthouse
Geneva, Illinois 60134
(Referral.)

Loop College
64 East Lake Street
Chicago, Illinois 60601
Paul Galvan
(Assistance to veterans.)

Malcolm X College
1900 West Van Buren Street
Chicago, Illinois 60612
Tony Johnson
(Service to veterans.)

Metro Vets Center
1100 Garfield Street
Oak Park, Illinois 60304
David B. Bingaman
(Readjustment counseling to eligible veterans.)

Midwest Biofeedback Institute
4316 Nutmeg Lane, Number 269
Lisle, Illinois 60532
Cheryl Koehler, Director
(Give support, do research, and provide therapy to veterans and families.)

National Association for the Advancement of Colored People
407 South Dearborn, Suite 1519
Chicago, Illinois 60605
Rev. Herbert Martin
(Information and referral.)

National Association of Black Veterans
c/o Gateway M.B. Church
1503 West Roosevelt Road
Chicago, Illinois 60608
Clem Henderson
(Uplifting of veterans educationally and intellectually.)

Operation PUSH
930 East 50th Street
Chicago, Illinois 60615
Rev. Willie Barrows
(Referral and outreach.)

United Steel Workers of America District 31
First National Bank Building
720 West Chicago Avenue
East Chicago, Illinois 46312
Rudy Nichols
(Labor union.)

Vets of Massachusetts
81 St. Nicholas Road
Framingham, Massachusetts 01701
Gail Steinecke
(Referral.)

Vet Center
5242 West Chicago Avenue
Chicago, Illinois 60618
Dave Eizinger, Earl Brown, George Vanodore,
Clem Henderson
(Counseling and referral for Vietnam era veterans.)

Veterans Affairs, Thornton College
15800 South State Street

South Holland, Illinois 60473
R. V. King
(Veterans' assistance.)

Veterans of Cincinnati
2674 Wendee Drive, Apt. 2347
Cincinnati, Ohio 45238
Tim Culvertson
(Counsel Vietnam veterans.)

Veterans of Elgin
330 Waters Street
Elgin, Illinois 60120
Paul Blecke
(Referral.)

Veterans of Michigan
3520 Monroe Street
Dearborn, Michigan 48124
Seth Suarez
(Referral.)

Veterans for Peace
542 South Dearborn, Room 510
Chicago, Illinois 60605
Michael Parisi
(To promote veterans' issues and peace.)

Vietnam Veterans Against the War
PO Box 20184
Chicago, Illinois 60620
Pete Zastrow, Barry Romo
(To organize veterans, especially Vietnam era
veterans, to meet needs.)

Vietnam Veterans of America, Inc.
329 8th Street, N.E.

Washington, D.C. 20002
John Terranzo
(Membership organization for Vietnam veterans.)

Vietnam Veterans of South Dakota
PO Box 2037
Rapid City, South Dakota 57709
Chris Johnson
(Counseling information on Agent Orange.)

Voters Registration Project
629 North Root Street
Aurora, Illinois 60505
Willie Collins
(Information regarding voter.)

T. C. King and Associates
300 North State Street, Suite 4705
Chicago, Illinois 60610
(Technical advisor.)

Veteran Employment Service
910 South Michigan Avenue
Chicago, Illinois 60605
(Government agency.)

Veterans Administration
536 South Clark Street
Chicago, Illinois 60605
John Hand
(Government agency.)

City of Chicago Department of Human Services
Office of Veterans Affairs
640 North LaSalle Street

Chicago, Illinois 60610
Cesar Rivera
(Veterans' programs.)

Chicago Urban League
2108 East 71st Street
Chicago, Illinois 60649
Rose Parker
(Voter registration.)

Maude DeVictor
50 West 71st Street, Apt. 511
Chicago, Illinois 60621
(Agent Orange information.)

Curtis Colin, Ph.D.
55 West Chicago Avenue
Oak Park, Illinois 60302
(Advisor regarding Vietnam veterans' readjustment.)

Montford Point Marines
312 East 75th Street
Chicago, Illinois 60619
Burt Potts

NATIONAL VETERANS TASK FORCE
ON AGENT ORANGE
National Office
P O Box 15972
St. Louis, Missouri 63114

MEMBERSHIP LIST
August 1980

Agent Orange Victims International
New York, New York

Agent Orange Advisory Committee
San Francisco, California

American Lutheran Church
Boston, Massachusetts

Association of Vietnam Veterans of Maryland
Baltimore, Maryland

Baton Rouge Association for Community Action
Baton Rouge, Louisiana

CAVEAT, Inc.
Champaign, Illinois

CCCO
Philadelphia, Pennsylvania

Citizens Against Toxic Herbicides
Clarkston, Washington

Missourians Against Toxins
University City, Missouri

National Association of Black Veterans
Milwaukee, Wisconsin

National Council of Churches
New York, New York

National Association of Concerned Veterans
Yukon, Oklahoma

National Veterans Law Center
Washington, District of Columbia

New Jersey Victims of Agent Orange
East Keansburg, New Jersey

Minnesota Veterans Coalition
St. Paul, Minnesota

Philadelphia Vets. Action Committee
Philadelphia, Pennsylvania

San Diegans Working Against Toxins
San Diego, California

Veterans Upgrade Center of New York
Brooklyn, New York

Vetline/Hotline
Highland Park, Illinois

Vietnam Era Veterans Association
Cambridge, Massachusetts

Vietnam Veterans Against the War
Milwaukee, Wisconsin

Vietnam Veterans of America
Washington, District of Columbia

Vietnam Veterans for Self Reliance
Hyannis, Massachusetts

Vietnam Veterans/Vietnam Victims
Philadelphia, Pennsylvania

Vietnam Veterans of South Dakota
Rapid City, South Dakota

INDEX

235